M000222116

Names Of Persons Who Took the Oath Of Allegiance to the State Of Pennsylvania

Edited by

JOHN B. LINN AND WM. H. EGLE, M.D.

Willow Bend Books

Willow Bend Books

65 East Main Street
Westminster, Maryland 21157-5026
1-800-876-6103

Source books, early maps, CDs—Worldwide

For our listing of thousands of titles offered
by hundreds of publishers see our website
<www.WillowBend.net>

Visit our retail store

Copyright © 1995, 2000 by Willow Bend Books

First Printed 1890

All rights reserved. No part of this book may be reproduced or transmitted
in any form or by any means, electronic or mechanical, including photocopying,
recording or by any information storage and retrieval system without written
permission from the author, except for the inclusion of brief quotations
in a review.

International Standard Book Number: 1-58549-306-6

Printed in the United States of America

HISTORICAL NOTE.

As early as May, 1776, the Continental Congress declared that it was "*irreconcilable to reason and good conscience that the American people should take the oaths for the support of government under the crown of Great Britain,*" and that it was "*necessary that every kind of authority under the crown should be suppressed.*" The struggle which ensued between those in the Proprietary interest, represented principally by the members of the Assembly, and the Whigs of the Revolution, was bitter, but the plan of the latter for the calling of a Convention was finally successful.

At a conference of the committees of observation for the different counties held at Carpenter's Hall's on the 18th of June, 1776, it was resolved that it "was necessary to call a Provincial Convention to form a new government in the authority of the people only, and the following religious test was proposed to the members threeof;

"*I, ———— ————, do profess in God the Father and in Jesus Christ His Eternal Son, the true God, and in the Holy Spirit one God blessed evermore, and do acknowledge the sacred Scriptures of the Old and New Testament to be given by Divine inspiration.*"

Notwithstanding the spirit of intolerance which actuated the adoption of this oath, immediate efforts were taken for a proper representation of every county in the State. The Convention met on the 15th of July, the members without hesitancy taking the prescribed test, and "during its session it not only discussed and perfected the measures necessary in the adoption of a Constitution, but assumed the supreme authority in the State, and legislated upon matters foreign to the object for which it was convened. Among other matters this body appointed a Council of Safety, to carry on the executive duties of the government, approved of the Declaration of Independence, and appointed justices of the peace who were required before assuming their functions to each take an oath of renunciation of the authority of George III, and one of allegiance to the State of Pennsylvania. The old Assembly which had adjourned on the 14th of June to meet on the 14th of August, could not obtain a quorum, and adjourned again to the 23d of September. It then interposed a feeble remonstrance against the invasion of its prerogatives by the Convention, but it was a dying protest. "The Declaration of Independence had given the old State Government a mortal blow, and it soon expired without a sigh—thus ending forever the proprietary and royal authority in Pennsylvania."—(WESTCOTT.)

The Constitution of 1776 went into immediate operation on its adoption, the 28th of September. The oath prescribed for members of Assembly was as objectionable as that required to be taken by the members of the Convention, and political disputes waged warm and bitter. The refusal of the State Navy Board, referred to in the minutes of that body, to take the oath of allegiance to the State, tended to increase the excitement, and this, with the disarrangement of the associators, required the adoption of more stringent measures.

The Legislature, by a general militia law, passed June 13, 1777, not only made full provision for the enrolment of all persons fit for military duty, but established a test and oath of allegiance, a measure highly necessary to restrain the insolence of the tories. The preamble and oath are in these words:

"WHEREAS, From sordid or mercenary motives, or other causes inconsistent with the happiness of a free and independent people, sundry persons have or may yet be induced to withhold their service and Allegiance from the Commonwealth of Pennsylvania as a free and independent State, as declared by Congress:

"AND WHEREAS, Sundry other persons in their several capacites have, at the risk of their lives and fortunes, or both, rendered great and eminent services in defence and support of the said independence, and may yet continue to do the same, and as both these sorts of persons remain at this time mixed, and in some measure undistinguished from each other, and the disaffected deriving undeserved service from the faithful and well affected:

"AND WHEREAS, Allegiance and protection are reciprocal, and those who will not bear the former are not nor ought to be entitled to the benefits of the latter:

"*Therefore it is enacted, etc.*, That all white male inhabitants of the State, except of the counties of Bedford and Westmoreland, above the age of eighteen years, shall, before the 1st day of the ensuing July, and in the excepted counties before the 1st day of August, take and subscribe before some justice of the peace an *oath* in the following form:

"*I,* ——————— ————————, *do swear (or affirm) that I renounce and refuse all allegiance to George the Third, king of Great Britain, his heirs and successors; and that I will be faithful and bear true allegiance to the Com-*

monwealth of Pennsylvania as a free and independent State, and that I will not at any time do or cause to be done any matter or thing that will be prejudicial or injurious to the freedom and independence thereof, as declared by Congress, and also, that I will discover and make known to some one justice of the peace of said State all treasons or traitorous conspiracies which I now know or hereafter shall know to be formed against this or any of the United States of America."

Severe penalties were imposed by this law on all who neglected or refused to take the oath. Many of the names which follow are those who took an active and prominent part in the revolutionary contest, and as a part of the history of that famous era, the record is worth preserving. It embraces but a small proportion, however, of the people of the State.

Not until the adoption of the Constitution of 1790 was the religious test dispensed with. The following lists, however, includes names (foreign born) of persons who took the oath after that period.

OATHS OF ALLEGIANCE.

—

We, the subscribers, do swear (or affirm) that we renounce and refuse all allegiance to George the Third, King of Great Britain, his heirs and successors, and that we will be faithful and bear true allegiance to the Commonwealth of Pennsylvania as a free and independent State, and that we will not at any time do, or cause to be done, any matter or thing that will be prejudicial or injurious to the freedom and independence thereof, as declared by Congress, and also that we will discover and make known to some one justice of the peace of the said State, all treasons and traitorous conspiracies which we now know or hereafter shall know to be formed against this or any of the United States of America.

June 20, 1777.

James Budden,
Samuel Caldwell,
William Davis,
Joseph Moulder,
John Leaboyteaus,
Edward Pole,

William Price,
Hugh Montgomery,
Henry Dougherty,
William Crispin,
Thomas Cuthbert, Jr.

June 21.

Thomas Pryor,
Thomas Fell,
Joseph Blewer,
John Hazelwood,
Thomas Washington,
John Brown,
Nathan Simmons,
Thomas Perkins,
Henry Spees,

Thomas Drummond,
Lauchlan McLean,
Thomas Hazelwood,
Griffith Jones,
Frazer Kinsly,
Benjamin Marshall,
William Blyth,
Samuel Levan,
Joseph Graysbury.

June 23.

Joseph Dean,
Captain John Ross,
Robert Eastburn,
Nathan Boys,
William Brown,
Joseph Penrose,

Paul Cox,
John Purviance,
Robert Handie,
Joseph Faning,
William McCullough,
Robert Barnhill,

Joseph Willson,
Thomas Bell,
Daniel Clymer,
David Jackson,
William Clark,
William Webb,
William Bartin,
Edward Cary Brown,

Baret Cantler,
John Wm. Annis,
Dennis Leary, Yeoman,
Peter Morgan,
Samuel Taylor,
Benjamin January,
Francis Daymon.

June 24.

James Mekemson,
Thomas Phillips,
Alexander Henderson,
William Marshall,
John Sneder,
Joseph Gamble,
Michael Dawson,
Robert Taggart,
Wingate Newman,
William Greenway,
Charles Miller,
Daniel Duncan,
James Cumings,
William Hall,
Anthony Cuthbert,
Nathaniel Allen,
Robert Smith,
John Reily, Esq.,
James Mease, Esq.,
Thomas Barclay,
Robert Brown,
Walter Shee,
John Earle,
Elijah Dow,
Philip Wert,
John Thompson,

Richard Brown,
John Kneis,
Jacob Kopp,
Isaac Wikoff,
Adam Weaver,
John Reily, Tobacconist,
Benjamin Hogeland,
Andrew Gordan,
Ephraim Bonham,
Adam Custard,
Jacob Brandt,
George Cooley,
James Pain,
Abraham Marko,
Frederick Hagner,
William Haverstick,
Nicholas Haverstick,
Adam Weaver,
James Longhead,
Edward Evans,
William Bonham,
Oswald Nauderhald,
James Roberts,
Charles Hammond,
Joseph Rhoads.

June 25.

Nathaniel Faulkner,
Robert Dill,
Lazarus Pine,
George Willson,
Ephraim Faulkner,
John Mitchell,
John Fullerton,
Casper Gayer.

Philip Moser,
Philip Flick,
William Shedacker,
John Beck,
Hugh Means,
Lodwick Sprogell,
Moses Young,
Edward Reyers,

Zacharia Hutchins,
Richard Bache,
Benjamin Connor.
Timothy Newman,
Adam Cleckner,
William Rush,
John Dean,
James Dundass,
John Dundass,
James Searle,
John Mease,
John King,
William Richards,
Thomas Bennett,
Christian Leonhard,
George Seitz,
Jacob Eckfield,
Christleb Barthug,
Peter Smick,
John Beck, Tailor,
William Ross,
James Bryson,
William Allen,
Joseph Carson,
Andrew Hodge,

Robert Logan,
John Cridland,
Robert Bridges,
Richard Redman,
Frederick Crout,
William Tharp,
Robert Gray,
William Dudley,
Joseph Foldwell,
Godfrey Sewing,
Jacob Bright,
John Mason,
Isaac Moses,
Daniel Stornmitz,
Alexander Plunkett,
Lawrence Lawlor,
Walter Corry,
James Morrison,
William Martin,
James Wharton,
George Garland,
John McFatrick,
John Sparhawk,
Robert Craig,
James Johnston.

June 26.

James Donnal,
Isaac Roach,
Jacob Masoner,
Samuel Blair,
Jacob Riffee,
John Hannah,
William Mason,
John Hall,
George Spangler,
Christian Pick,
Jacob Beunighoff,
Hugh Fraser,
Michael Halling,
Robert McKnight,
Jacob Hans,
George Felkner,
Joseph Hubley,
Peter Stoy,
John Willson,

William Hall, Cooper,
Peter Hegner,
David Thompson,
John Shee,
Christian Gally,
Robert Morris, Esq.,
James Willson, Esq.,
Richard Peters, Esq.,
George Clymer, Esq.,
David Beveridge,
Peter Conver,
Jacob Clyver,
William Milnor,
Joseph Johnston,
Alexander Gardner,
Henry Miller, Printer,
Henry Haller,
Henry Martin,
James Josiah,

John Handley,
George Kelso,
Daniel Goodman,
Michael Rankinhorn,
John Thompson,
George Lohrman,
George Price,
David Crotty,
John Claypoole,
William McIlhinny,
Frederick Zahn,
Gailack Haas,
Charles Stewart,
Thomas Gregory,

Josiah James,
Robert Cather,
Nicholas Weaver,
Michael Immel,
Matthew Irwin,
James Read,
William Peel,
Conrad Meyerly,
Frederick Lutz,
Philip Rice,
John George,
William Harmon,
John Nixon.

June 27.

Philip Springer,
Christian Strealy,
Henry Ernest,
John Frederick Lirich,
Michael Stemner,
Michael Goodman,
Michael Anthoney,
James Bray,
Philip Sedleman,
William Henry,
William Haysham,
William Smith,
George Worts,
Martin Wort,
John Patterson,
Joseph Marsh,
Thomas Tyllyer,
Jeremiah Fisher,
Jacob Clous,
William Miller,
John North,
Abraham Marshall,
John Emmes,
John Ashmead,
Michael Shoemaker,
Cornelius Sweers,
John Montgomery,
Philip Hagner,
Daniel Summers,
John Campbell,

Samuel Massey,
Norton Pryor,
Frederick Lirich,
Alexander Crawford,
Charles West,
Jacob Young,
Jacob Hare,
George Houston,
Francis Buck,
Isaac Cox,
Alexander Nesbitt,
John Brown,
Peter Gallagher,
James Bennett,
Joseph Crawford,
Christian Kinsley,
Richard Butler,
John Reibolt,
Stephen Cronin,
Michael McGannon,
Tobias Keen,
Joseph Brown,
William Hammon,
John Little,
Henry Peters,
Henry Mayer,
Ludwig Kacher,
Adam Guire,
John Hawtyn,
John Deal,

Cuthbert Landers,
Martin Rably,
John Pryor,
John Wager,
Thomas Read,
Michael Uber,
Valentine Rees,
Thomas Peters,
Manuel Eyer,
Michael Shriver,
John Michelwain,
John Omley,
Peter Summer,
Godfrey Rapp,
Fred'k Marcus Montelus,
Frederick Myer,
Andrew Caldwell,
James Caldwell,
George Sheppard,
Philip Stimble,

David Allison,
William Bunting,
Thomas Silvester,
Philip Flack,
Frederick Powell,
Adam Yeager,
Christian Fite,
Michael Underlea,
Henry Jones,
Philip Megar,
George Smith,
Godfrey Hawker,
William Hudson,
Thomas Butler,
Benjamin Gorman,
Jacob Weaver,
Nicholas Stimble,
Thomas Townsend,
George Lechlor,
William Keates,

June 28.

Joseph Toy,
John Kitler,
Levy Budd,
John Parker,
Gottlieb Roll,
George Forepaugh,
Lambert Cadwalleder,
Wollery Meng,
Joseph Campbell,
John Comegys,
Jonathan Gostelowe,
Peter Snider,
John Hoffman,
John Hall,
Thomas Huggins,
Jacob Henry,
Henry Magg,
William McColough,
Samuel Sutton,
Adam Thompson,
Joseph Ferguson,
Silas Engles,
William Allen.

Paletiah Webster, Jr.,
Samuel Proctor,
James McCullem,
Christopher Neterfield,
Lewis Grant,
Nicholas Brooks,
Philip Dover,
Peter Gardener,
John Suter,
Jacob Feit,
Thomas Jones,
Christopher Henkle,
Christian Wilker,
Martin Evans,
John O'Bryan,
Henry Jones,
Ruloff Alberson,
Benjamin Tower, Esq.,
Peter Letelier,
Thomas Preston,
Conrad Way,
Thomas Rue,
Joseph Stewart,

Matthew Strong,
Charles Cherykee,
Thomas Leland,
Peter Grinion,
William Simple,
William Potts,
John Morel,
Herman Chappel,
Frederick Bird,
Henry Hill, Esq.,
Robert Mullen,
Thomas Howell,
James Brown,
William Jones,
Isaac Gardner,
James Carroll,
Conrad Miller,
Charles Allen,
John Lushet,
Philip Spilman,
Jeremiah Lewis,
John Jackson,
Conrad Firestone,
Samuel Lyons,
Ludwig Kuhn,
William Pool,
John Donnally,
John Farr,
John Whiteman,
George Stoots,
William Robinson,
Michael Farner,

John Wharton, Esq.,
Abraham Fox.
William White, Clerk,
Benjamin Rush,
Robert Purdy,
Edward Dowling,
David DeBarthot,
John McFadden,
George Graham,
James Rowan,
Hugh Hodge,
Blathwaite Jones,
William Alricks,
William Kerlin,
John Caman,
John Cappel,
George Jackson,
Eneas Skillinger,
James Jnee,
Daniel Menertie,
Peter Young,
Jacob Martin,
William Burkhart,
Frederick Cammeloe,
Daniel Stever,
Frederick Shimcastle,
George Smith,
Richard Oates,
John Osborn,
Thomas Ingles,
Charles Massey.

June 30.

William Drenry,
John Priest,
Jeremiah Cullin,
Garrett Hulsekamp,
James Wood,
Frederick Sumfield,
Daniel Cross,
Philip Reybold,
Thomas Denham,
Matthias Stimble,
John Craft,

Charles Kokanterfer,
Joseph Gaven,
Paul Paul,
Jacob Demend,
George Berry,
William Blake,
Daniel Nodel,
Peter Bingham,
John Buzhart,
William Pitt,
John Blake,

Jacob Kline,
John Butler,
Whitehead Humphreys,
William Kenly,
Christopher Hartrenfft,
Leonard Hartrenfft,
George Douglass,
John Osman,
William Malone,
Joseph Fawlon,
Solomon Wright,
Thomas Maro,
James Barker,
William Pain,
George Edwards,
John McGill,
David Bang,
Valentine Gallaspy,
Michael Kremer,
Frederick Merker,
George Lesher,
Adam Moledore,
Joseph Harkmonder,
Jacob A. Howell,
Benjamin George Eyre,
Charles Souder,
James Carter,
Benjamin Davis, Jr.,
Archibald Burns,
Thomas Kane,
Henry Lee,
Daniel Smith,
Bethana Hodgkinson,
Robert Jones,
Samuel Williams,
John Hackatt,
Philip Ardla,
John Tyler,
George Cochran,
John McKinnay,
Adam Hoffman,
Charles Craswell,
John Swan,
John Cochran,
Richard Kinly,
Joshua Stuttson,

Henry Kurtz,
James C. Nicklass,
James Chabaud,
William Side,
Henry Rabsom,
Paul Figner,
George White,
John Devow,
Benjamin Davis, Surgeon,
Joseph Tatem,
Robert Croft,
Joseph Fineur,
Martin Burkhart,
George Justice,
Godfrey Hiney,
Daniel Mullen,
John Cox,
Jacob Houser,
William Main,
John Miley,
John Specht,
James Dougherty,
Leonard Lutz,
John Totton,
George Stout,
John Light,
Samuel Hooke,
Samuel McClure,
Daniel Butler,
Thomas Denniston,
Andrew Suplee,
James Mathers,
Thomas Beal,
John McCartey,
John Bergman,
Philip Mous,
John Westcott,
Mathias Cline,
Philip Cline,
Peter Pullin,
Daniel Badger,
John Vanusin,
John Wild,
Jacob Ron,
David McElmoyl,
Rudolph Lehr,

William Boyd,
Nathaniel Norgrove,
George Nunemaker,
John Chaplin,
James Ham,
Thomas Millard,
Andrew Hertzog,
Jacob Rubsom,
George Ingram,
Paul Bearns,
Henry Smith,
John Knight,
Peter Hellam,
Francis McClister,
Patrick Branum,
Joseph Quality,
Thomas Bradford,
Joseph Bond,
Baldur Rabuns,
Thomas Leiper,
Peter Trites,
John Hoffman,
Thomas Sartan,
Henry Jonas,
Adam Smith,
John Jacob,
William Tuckey,
Charles Parcival,
Thomas Shaw,
George Carlinger,
Philip Burke,
John Stroup,
Peter Worrell,
Nathan Jones,
William Maris,
Jeremiah Andrews,
Michael Duff,
David Richardson,
James Brown,
George Honey,
James Welsh,
Philip Willimore,
John Walker,
John Ashburn,
Allen McCollum,
Lewis Bryant,
Albertus Popplesdorf,
Joseph Plowman,
John Duche,
George Peddle,
Jonathan Harned,
Edward McKaige,
Jacob Grantham,
William Kope,
Philip Vernes,
John Biddle,
Jeremiah Much,
Charles Lawton,
Andrew Nelson,
Warwick Hale,
John Blyth,
Arthur Campbell,
John Figel,
James Monks,
John Hudle,
John Painter,
Griffith Griffiths,
James Little,
Samuel Lowery,
Christopher Miller,
Thomas Patton,
Henry Barber,
Francis Corcoran,
William How,
James Spriggs,
John Grant,
William Anderson,
John Ogborn,
John Koch,
Martin Minhold,
Samuel Stewart,
Christopher Martin,
John Reynolds,
James Erwin,
Christopher Kneas,
Andrew Young,
James Wells,
Thomas Harper,
Thomas Stiles,
John Pringle,
Jno. Maxwell Nesbitt,
Thomas Bryant.

July 1.

Robert Maffet,
Richard Sewell,
William Suringhousen,
Benj. Condy,
George Wood,
George Whiteall,
George Brigs,
Robert Fleming,
Francis Hopkinson, Esq.,
Philip Ecker,
Thomas Crispin,
John Swain,
Henry Neil,
James Lavers,
Charles Forder,
George Parker,
Frederick Schler,
George Thum,
John Deldine,
James Smart,
James McGlew,
Conrad Young,
Nicholas Egan,
Reese Peters,
George Senneff,
Valentine Bayer,
John Hamilton,
Clement Humphreys,
John Souder,
Daniel Dick,
John Cox,
John Johnson,
Christopher Bradley,
Seth Griffing,
Benjamin King,
Maurice Rogers,
Henry Baags,
Michael Davenport,
Patrick Crogan,
Frederick Dick,
Daniel McMenamen.
Thomas McCullem,
Samuel McCoogan,

John Hannah,
James Gibson,
James Elliot,
Adam McConnell,
John McPharson,
William Rigdon,
Plunket Fleeson,
John Ferguson,
Alexander Nelson,
Jacob Abel,
Frederick Steelman,
George Enson,
John Banon,
John Fromberger,
William Morris,
Jacob Shreder,
Stephen Foreman,
Francis Lusher,
Frederick Hoffman,
Thomas Morgan,
John Drinker,
Isaac White,
Jonathan Iszard,
James Gibson,
William Fishbourne,
Champion Wood,
Hugh Hodge, Jr.,
James Reed,
Robert Mordock,
John Sowerwalt,
George Middaugh,
Jonathan Arnold,
Robert Allen,
Past Hamilton,
Joseph White,
Francis Harris,
Daniel Drais,
Robert Crumbie,
Anthony Hodgkinson,
Samuel Davis,
William Allibone,
Manuel Josephson,
Solomon Meyers Cohen.

July 2.

Michael Onongst,
John Crawford,
Charles Lyon, Jr.,
William Carter,
George Jacob Housman,
Godfrey Spangle,
Samuel Alexander,
George Taylor,
James Edward Finley,
Jacob Meyers,
Philip Cripts,
Richard Inkson,

Charles Freeman,
John Pullin,
Daniel Maloney,
Thomas Story,
Robert Haron,
John Gavaran,
George Seller,
John Brown,
Jacob Baker,
James Gregory,
Bartholomew Baker,
John Burket,

July 3.

John Neglee,
Philip Buck,
Stephen Tler,
Robert Brewton,
James Sayers,
James Forbes,
John Taylor,
John McKinney,
Patrick Moore.
John Harrison.
Samuel Smith,

William Davey,
Anthony Butler,
James O'Bryan,
Melcher Loven,
Samuel Ward,
Adam Ritchie,
Charles Foster,
Richard Johnston,
Jacob Coffman,
Leonard Stoneburner.

July 4.

Alexander Campbell,
Joseph Bradford,
Charles Cartwright,
John Donaldson,
Blair McClenachan,
William Hamilton,
Conrad Gray,
Richard Knowles,
Francis Bennett,
Jacob Painter,
Moses Myers,
Theophilus Parke,
David Smith,
Samuel North,

Thomas Foster,
Balzer Trout,
Christopher Flowers,
Adam Cassey,
Joseph Dorvill.
David Hunon,
John Ewing, the Reverend,
Daniel King,
Francis Harrison,
John Ord, Jr.,
Robert Tatnall,
Benjamin Rue,
John Jarvis.

July 5.

Abraham Mason,
William Burk,
Christopher Lochner,

Samuel Boucher,
John Hodgson,
John Brayfield,

William Harris,
Christopher Caul,
James Dunn,

George Donal,
Nathaniel Cope,
Anthony McQueston,
Emanuel Rouse,
David Hall,
Samuel Leacock,
Mathias Landerberger,
Benjamin Boyant,
Ludwick Sengtus,

Thomas Lawrence,
Francis Stewart,
Tobias Bougher,
John Leiser,

Lawrence Barry,
Isaac Austin,
Andrew Leiper,
Francis Gurney,

William Eckart,
Peter Lowery,
Henry Piper,
Frederick Sent,
Nicholas Burr,
James Bowles,

Jasper Corrie,
Arthur Higgins,
William Chatwin,

Joseph Barry,
Isaac Lort,
Peter Evans,
Robert Hopkins,
John Kinsly,
Theodorous Barry,
Frederick Ran,
Norris Copper,
Jacob Wynkoop,

William Palmer,
Charles Redding,
Richard Powell,

July 7.

Joseph Williams,
William Fisher,
Adam Grubb,
James Skinner,
William Woodhouse,
Andrew Casil,
Joseph Buck,
Thomas Shields,
George Heytch.

July 8.

Mathias Kelly,
John Yentzer,
John Newman,
Eneas Murry.

July 9.

William Shaw,
John Feeston,
Parsons Clark,
John Beacher.

July 10.

Hugh Willson,
Thomas Moore,
Capt. John Webb,
Joseph Sau ders,
Thomas Clear,
Samuel Howell, **Jr.**

July 11.

William Allison,
Jeremiah Simmons,
Charles Moore.

July 12.

Isaac Williams,
Peter Primmer,
Adam Primmer,
Thomas Learning,
James Glasgow,
Anthony Ammon,
Adam Handle,
Samuel Nicholas, Esq.,
Thomas Rowan.

Presley Blackiston,
Henry Hawkinson,

Isaac Corson,
Peter Drummond,
William Dibley,

Robert McMullen,
Jeremiah Johnston,

William Roberts,
Lawrence Purfield,
William Hanson,
Owen Ashton,

Robert Rennet,
Peter Haws,
Matthew Musgrove,
Josiah Robinson,
Peter Bruster,
Peter Robinson,
John Christie,
William Rolston,
James White,

Isaac Jones,
James Creighton,
John Patterson,
James Smith,

Stephen Lowery,
John Bazalee,

William Moore,

James McGuire,
Michael Fulloro,
Thomas Marle,

Christian Kunkel.

Nicholas Fitzsimons,
  2—Vol. III.

July 14.
John Murdock,
James Barr.

July 15.
Thomas Clarkson,
Gear Chadwick,
Wm. Watson.

July 16.
Samuel Ford.

July 17.
John Duffield,
Silas Watts,
Robert Henry.

July 18.
James McCrea,
Robert Cottenham,
Samuel Dolby,
Samuel Caskey,
George Farflar,
David Blid,
George Shiets,
Christopher Bender.

July 21.
John Richards,
William Hunter,
John Eckstein,
Thomas Fanen.

July 22.
William Nicholason.

July 23.
Jonathan Hufty.

July 24.
John Knowles,
William Watkin.

July 25.

July 26.
Benjamin Bickerton.

Joe Cæsar, a free negro,
William Smith,
Thomas Hart,
Joseph Faulkner,

James Mitchell.

Peter Merckel,
Thomas Shed,

Richard Lees,
Samuel Bush,
Aaron Hunter,
Daniel McCaracher,
William Crispin,
Robert Eachus,
William Gardner,

Jacob Holton,
John Holmes,

James Stell,

James Laird,

Moses Moses,
Andrias Bentinger,
James Moydes,
Samuel Meredith, Esq.,
Edward Paschall,

Hezekiah Kimble,

Wiliam Lyell,
Jacob Zoll,

Jacob Haltzhimer,

John Strimbeck.

John Ladd Howell.

July 28.

Nehemiah Mall,
Thomas Black,
Samuel Black,
David Thurston.

July 29.

July 30.

Daniel Elliott,
John Luger.

July 31.

George Goodwin,
Richard Humphrey, Esq.,
Robert Bethell,
Josiah Harned,
Peter Hulick,
James Armstrong,
Frederick Heiler.

August 4.

John Jackston.

August 5.

John Steward.

August 6.

August 7.

John Taggort,
Frederick Mopps,
Patrick Dugan,
Adam Martin.

August 9.

August 11.

Joshua Hatfield.

August 13.

Peace Wademan.

August 14.

August 15.

August 16.

John Wilson Hustin,
William Watson,

Philip Lacy.

August 18.

Isaac Ely,
Nicholas Nailor,

James Thompson,
Robert Can.

August 19.

Thomas Moore,
Thomas Cunningham,

John Cunningham,
Joseph West.

August 21.

William Sturgeon,
Michael Wells,
Thomas Cuthbert,
John Ledru,
Benjamin Cross

Jacob Proby,
George Meyers,
Joseph Musgrave,
Philip Maguire,
'James Sutter.

August 27.

William Parker.

August 28.

Edward York.

August 29.

Edward Oxley.

August 30.

Charles Risque,
Isaac Bellanger,
Robert Aitken,

Samuel McClain.
Ely Few,
Robert Owen.

September 1.

John Martin,
James Kirkpatrick,
Lucas Walraven,
John Lewis,

Henry Finner,
Jonathan Beers,
William Sellars.

September 2.

Andrew Stanwood,
Jacob Hibbart,

Isaac Trask.

September 3.

John Brown,
George Kimley,
Henry Wynkoop,
Richard Dowdel,

Paul Roberts,
Nicholas Ribbel,
Conrad Smith.

September 4.

Griffith Levering,
John Jenkins,
John Nordon,

Pain Newman,
Caleb Emblen.

September 5.

Mary Thompson,
Thomas Dorsey,

Samuel Garrigues,
Thomas Palmer.

September 6.

Christian Tiley,
Thomas Leech,
John Dennis,

Casper Wittepack,
Daniel Haines,
John Haines.

September 8.

William Love,
Andrew Carson,

John Boyle,
James Robinson.

September 9.

Solomon Robinson,
William Rogers,

James Duncan,
Michael Hopkins.

September 10.

Ludwick Wiser,
George Madery,
Samuel Currey,
James Kennedy,

Robert Wall,
Joseph Ball,
Isaac Shoemaker.

September 11.

William Taylor,
James Short,

Luke Matthewan,
George Rolston.

September 12.

Cornelius O'Niel,
Edmond Sweney,
John Leshay,
John Fitch,

Aaron Musgrave, **Jr.**,
James Cobourn,
John Reed,
William Connell.

September 13.

John McDonnell,
William Hughes,
John Harding,
Henry Friday,
William Brooks,

Alexander Armstrong,
Robert Bedison,
George Robinson,
James Adair.

September 14.

Robert Whitehill, Esq.,
William Brown,
David Harris,

Robert Morris, **Mulatto,**
Jacob Bouldin,
Henry Doran.

September 15.

John Story,
William Thorton,
Robert Patton,
Richard Mason.
James Dow,
George Arthur,

William Young,
William Young, **Jr.**,
James Heanes,
Richard Hackett,
Thomas Haley.

September 16.

Morris Roach,   John Cottle.

September 18.

Zebadiah David.   John Adams.

September 19.

Elias Pew,   George Barns.
Bastian Stonemeyer,

September 22.

William Kennedy,   Andrew Murrey.

November 15.

William McFadem,   Reese Meredith.

June 24, 1778.

Thomas William, Esq.,   Edward Shippen.
Samuel Powell, Esq.,

June 25.

Richard Willing,   Tench Cox,
Alexander Wilcock, Esq.,   Thomas Asheton,
James Allen, Esq..   Stephen Collins,
Doct. Thomas Bond,   Matthew McHugh.

June 26.

John Knor, Cooper,   Jacob Harman,
William McMurtrie,   John Boutcher,
William Shaw, Cooper,   Michael Doogan,
William Smith, Reverd. Docr., Doctor John Redman,
William Constable,   John Cobourn.
Jacob Myer,

June 27.

George Heytle,   William Sitgreaves,
Peter Cooper,   Mark Freeman,
Philip Heyle,   Asheton Humphreys,
—— Davies,   John Keble,
Curtis Clay,   John Hood,
Richard Rundle,   James Seagrove,
Thomas Murgatroyd,   Thomas Gray,
Jonathan Meredith,   Captain James Cockran.
John Evans,   John Lawrence, Esq.,
Joseph Leblence,   Henry Gurney.
William Tricket,

June 29.

Richard Footman,   John Nicholson,
Henry Marks,   John Jones,
Joseph Shewell,   John Martin,

James Fudge,
Charles Woollful,
Phineas Harlan,
James Morton,
Eneas Urguhart,
Levy Hollingsworth,
Samuel Murdock,
William Beavan,

Evan Evans,
James Curtin,
John Marshall,
Joseph Swift,
John Shields,
George Douglass,
Alexander Corbet.

June 30.

Richard Wister, Jr.,
John Wister, Jr.,
William Chancellor,
Roger Flahavan,
George Hauton,
John Grant,
Michael Owner,
Samuel Inglis,
Nathan Cook,
John Smith,
Nicholas Brooks,
Joseph Thornhill,
John Andrew Messersmith, Jr.,
Dennis Dougherty,
James Reynolds,
James Sparks,
Moses Cox,
Samuel Read,
Richard Freeman,

Benjamin Morgan,
George Grimes,
Peter Kurtz,
Archibald McCall,
Henry Ash,
Stephen Shewell,
Samuel Crawford,
Joseph Stamper,
George James,
Jacob Rutter,
John Sullivan,
John Stamper,
Elias Botner,
Peter Thompson,
Thomas Thompson,
Samuel Covell,
Alexander Tod,
Robert Bond,
Jesse Jones.

July 1.

Edward Bleakney,
Peter Sutter,
John Haines,
James Conchy,
John Wells,
William Harris,
James Scott,
James Roche,

Patrick McGinnes,
Joseph Ledrue,
Robert Morton,
Joseph Donaldson,
Lawrence Powell,
Barnabas Higgins,
Jonathan Brown,
John Rouking.

July 2.

William Craig,
John Steel,
Thomas Clark,
Francis Eskillion,
Edward Moore,
Jacob Weis,

George Litzenberger,
John Sellars,
Garrald Forrister,
Peter Wade,
Charles Stedman.

July 3.

Charles Wharton,
Isaac Wharton,
Thomas Meredith,
Carpentar Wharton,
Sam'l Lewis Wharton,
Daniel Evans,
Joseph Turner, Esq.,
James Hendry,
Samuel Kelsey,
William Read,

Charles Hurst,
Nicholas Hart,
John Olden,
Adam Myrtetus,
Samuel Hudson,
Abraham Levy,
Alexander Morrison,
Isaac Worrell,
John Chavalier.

July 4.

James Richards,
Henry Vanreid,
Sam'l McKean,
John Mifflin,

Benjamin Chew, Esq.,
Benjamin Chew, Jr.,
Benjamin Meyers,
William Harper,

July 6.

Robert Strettle Jones,
Conrad Baker,
Adam Anderson,
James Hunter,

John Harland,
David Pancost,
Patrick Byrne,
Robert Parrish.

July 7.

Samuel Seivertt,
Robert Cocks,
John Barnes,
John Parrish, Jr.,
John Philip Miller,
Stephen Moore,
James Vaux,
William Lawrence,

Thomas Davis,
Samuel Walker,
Charles Edwards,
Philip Benezett,
Christian Fahns,
Joseph Parks,
Thomas Hemphill,
John Lawrence.

July 8.

Nathaniel Walton,
Hugh Miller,
Robert Wharton,
Thomas Lake,
David Ware,
John Howard,
Blase Boyer,
John Hall,
John Groves,
The Honorable John Penn,

Joseph Stransbury,
Joseph Turner, Jr.,
John Fustian,
David Fen,
Philip Faulkrode,
Phelim Mackerson,
John Ackroyd,
Thomas Wright,
James Grayson.

July 9.

Benjamin Herning,
Samuel Jefferys,

Thomas Montgomery
John Thomas,

Adam Hubley,
Josiah Matlock,
Jacob Hart,

Morgan Ridge,
James Singleton,
Richard Thomas,
John Clarke,
Bernard Fearis,
James Tilghman,
William Forbes,

John Mendorfelth,
James McClearen,
Samuel Story,

James Craig,
Timothy Carroll,
William Ogden,
John Sibbald,
William Morrell,
John Wood,
Robert Priest,
John Levins,

John Miller,
David Cunning,
Jacob Shoemaker,

John Palmer,
Matthew Felles,
Jonathan Barington,

Joseph Fawcett,
Robert McNair,
Townsend White,

Alexander Carr, Jr.,
Robert Harris,
Jacob Neglee,
John Deighton,
Job Butcher,

Thomas Will. Pierce,
Philip Wiseman,

James Egleson,
Isaac Kelly.

July 10.

Abraham Chovet, Doct. **Phys.**,
Ephraim Clark,
Thomas Mendenhall,
Daniel Benezett,
Pelatiah Webster,
Jacob Cohen.

July 11.

Jacob Bumm,
John Knox.

July 13.

Robert Hazelhurst,
Joseph Swabey,
Bryon O'Harrah,
Abraham Dehaven,
John Weaver,
Jeremiah Smith,
Frederick Kesselman.

July 14.

David Mellin,
William Webb.

July 15.

George Dickvendorf,
John Rudolph.

July 16.

Jacob Myers,
John Barron.

July 17.

Henry Wilson,
Matthew Pratt,
John Dowers,
Thomas Betagh.

July 18.

Chamless Allen,
Henry Kurtz,

Samuel Wells,
Philip Ling,
James Hartley,
William Givin,
Patrick Magarge,
Daniel Sower,

John Solter,

Bowyer Brooks,
Patrick Hogan,

Daniel Lester,
David Franks,
Archibald Stewart,

David Lenox,
James Herron,
Joseph Fox,
Jacob Bury,

Nathaniel Ashley,
Christian Minich,
Godfrey Twelves,
Philip Ling,

Wm. Bohannon,
Joseph Hunter,
Jacob Trump,
John Trump,
Andrew Tibout,

Isaac Vanost,
Samuel Williams,
John Cox, Jr.,
John Hall,
Griffith Jones,
James Callahan,

Charles Finney,
David Lapsley,
Thomas Davis,
Duncan Stewart,
John Slatery,
James Talbot,

Robert Coe,
Jacob Reese,
Daniel Forbes,
Thomas Byrnes,
James Cooper.

July 22.
Benjamin Cottman.

July 23.
Daniel Dupuy.

July 24.
William Sykes,
Joseph Morris.

July 25.
Richard Porter,
Isaac All,
William Sellars, **Jr.**

July 27.
William Meredith,
Isaac Abraham,
Joseph Fox.

July 28.
William Dewees,
Andrew Mattern,
Christopher Myrtetus,
John Dugan.

July 29.
George Miller,
Conrad Coleman,
John Salter,
Thomas Claridge,
Bartholomew Sutton,
James Sharwood.

July 30.
Jacob Christler,
Joseph Craig,
Andrew Wright,
James Bell,
Joseph Gee.

Patrick Martin,
Thomas Stewart,
Edward Hannah,

Amos Sturgis.

James Glenn,
Eleazer Truber,
Edward Miles,

Jacob Beckley,
Charles Stine,
Richard Lynell,
William Leich,
George Stevens,
Tobias Fisher,
James Megettegen,

William Straker,

William Seddons,

William Morris,
John Dilworth,
Henry Heneman,

Thomas Peters,
Patrick Loughan,

James Betson,
Thomas Brown,
Henry Bickley,

John Tittermary,

Alexander Fullerton,

Joseph Traxeller,
George Horne,
John Staple,

July 31.
John Williams,
Joseph Lyndall,
Peter Simmonson.

August 1.

August 3.
Benjamin Coates,
William Pald,
Anthony Yeldall.

August 4.
John Taylor,
Francis Kroasen,
John Welsh.
Evan Thomas,
Isaac Green, Jr.,
Joseph Robinson.

August 6.
Samuel Young.

August 7.

August 8.
Robert Collings,
Edward Cutbush.

August 10.
Joseph Huddle.

August 12.
Lawrence Bickley,
Francis Weller,
Philip McCardell.

August 13.
William Karr.

August 14.
Matthew Johns.

August 15.
Henry Lentz,
Lewis Micke.

August 17.

Amos Whitson,
James Fletcher,
William McDowell,
Brian Barker,
Robert Bonner,

Gasper Guyger,
Sebastian Neil,
Charles Conkler,
Christian Fugher.

August 19.

Peter Wikoff,
Joseph Shippen,
John Brubaker,

Joseph Duffield,
Joseph Foster,
John Helt.

August 20.

William Ball,
John Taylor,

Lemuel Savage.

August 22.

John Fisher,
Nathan Cotman,
Jacob Utree,

Isaac Busby,
William Edwards,
Alexander Hunter.

August 24.

Joseph Ashton,
John Johnston,
Elias Toy,
Peter Henderson,
James Wood,
Samuel Adams,

Lawrence Vance,
Samuel Goff,
Charles Eustace,
Samuel Garrett,
Daniel Williams.

August 25.

William Moland,
Lewis Ward,

Silas Crispin,
Joseph Davis.

August 26.

Thomas Ashton,
Lawrence Johnston,
Isaac Willard,
Philip Maynagh,
Joseph Claypoole,
Richard Tittermerry,

Philip Willson,
James Abercombie,
Isaac Coates,
Joseph Sans,
Richard Farmer.

August 27.

George Mifflin,

James Brown.

August 28.

Thomas Franklin,
Archibald McDermot,

Peter Feneick,
Thomas Bristol.

August 29.

Lardner Clarke,
Jacob Vanosten,
Jacob Johnson,
Michael Engle,

Thomas Goff,
Jacob Weaver,
Daniel McNaff,
James Willson.

August 31.

Benjamin Engle,
Thomas Crispin.
John Snyder,
Heym Solomon,
John David Sickle,

Robert Duncan,
John Marshall,
Samuel Judah,
John Dowenhime,
Francis Mahony.

September 2.

John Welsh,

Joseph Willis.

September 3.

Alexander Holmes,
Joshua Collins,
John Stille,
Edward Kirby,
Joseph Holdstock,
Edward McGill,
Alexander Foster,

John Foulke,
Peter Whiteside,
Samuel Henesey,
James Bremner,
Hugh Law,
Frederick Hasler,
George Seitz.

September 10.

THOMAS MIFFLIN, Esq., he also produced a qualification taken before General Gates to the United States, agreeeable to the resolves of Congress, on the 29th last March.

THOMAS MIFFLIN.

William Coats. Sadler,
Nathan Nichols,

Septimus Coats,
Stephen Champaign.

September 11.

William West, Jr., Esq.,
Peter Scull, Esq.,

James Crawford.

September 14.

Peter Sunlider,
Isaac Jones,

James King.

September 15.

Theophilus Gardner,

Henry Lalor, **Hatter.**

September 16.

Robert Hagan.

September 17.

James Jeffreys.

September 19.

Nicholas Bernard,
George Reed,

Robert Erwin.

September 21.

John Leech,

Henry Lockhead.

September 22.

Samuel Corry, a Pruss.
Capt. John Green,

William Poyntill,
Philip Super.

James Cordill,   Jacob Charles.
Richard Farmer,

September 23.

Peter Carmich.

September 24.

Lieut. Col. George North.

September 26.

Stacy Hepburn,   John Blake.
Jonathan Penrose,

September 28.

Peter Larot,   James Tempest,
George Catton,   William Batt,
Samuel Miles, Esq.,   Frederick McConn.

September 29.

James Sheward.

September 30.

Joseph Norman.

October 3.

Peter Conver,   Sam'l Cadwallader Morris.
Cadwallader Morris,

October 5.

Robert Sherer,   ·   Thomas Jennings, Esq.

October 6.

Robert Correy,   Samuel Howell.

October 7.

John Valentine Gaul,   Samuel Head.

October 8.

Abraham Cohan,   William Leaver.

October 9.

James Davis,   Joseph Reed, Esq.

October 10.

John Flick,   Joseph Mitchell.

October 12.

John Browne,   Benjamin Dean.
Stephen Beard,

October 13.

John Cadwallader, Esq.,   John Byrne,
James Duncan,   Jacob Benighoff,
Michael Vancourt,   James Vanuxen.

October 16.

Reynold Wharton.

October 17.

William Tilton, prisoner.

October 19.

Henry White, Physich.

October 20.

Evan Edwards.

October 21.

John Taylor, mariner.

October 27.

Stephen Girard.

October 30.

William Stretch,   Archibald **Gardner.**

October 31.

Francis Ellis.

November 4.

Jesse Guyger.

November 6.

Patrick Brown.

November 7.

Jacob Leibenzeter,   Major Thomas Lambert **Byles.**
Jeremiah Horton, Gent.,

November 9.

Joseph Graysbury.

November 11.

John Kipple.

November 16.

William Hembel,   Solomon **Solomons.**
Christ'r Kelby Allecock,

November 19.

Daniel Borman.

November 20.

James Gibbon, Lieutenant.

November 21.

Henry Callaghan

November 23.

John Parker.

November 24.

Matthias Gometz,   Jacob **Souder.**
Moses Judah,

November 25.

Cap. Jno. Richardson, prisoner, Cap. Dan'l Broadhead, Jr., pris-
Cap. Andrew Forrest, prisoner, oner.

The Names of Those that Have Taken the Oath of Fidelity Before Me, Together with the Years, Months and Days of the Months when Taken, pr. Me, HUGH MARTIN, Esq.

September ye 11, 1777. Samuel Glasgow.

23,   John Giffin.

23,   Moses Lotta.

23.   Samuel Robinson.

23,   Alexander Maxwell.

23,   Samuel Serrels.

24,   Isaac Miller.

26,   Jacob McClain.

October ye 3, 1777. Isaac McHendry.

3,   Joseph Hutchison.

9,   Clements McGerry.

9,   Joseph Eager.

9,   William Robinson.

9,   James McQuiston.

9,   John Kilgore.

10,   George Latimer.

13,   Robert Waddle.

13,   John Robinson.

13,   James Martin.

14,   John Moore, Esq.

14,   Alexander Young.

14,   John Brandon.

14,   Robert Robinson.

14,   William Young.

14,   Charles Siskey.

14,   Robert Jamison.

14,   Abraham Leasure,

14,   David Perry.

14,   John Cortney.

14,   James Waddle.

14,   Francis McGinnice.

14,   John Stuchal.

November ye 1, 1777. William Ferguson.

1,   James Ferguson.

1,   John Jack.

1   John Speelman.

1,   James Clark.

3,   George Sulear.

3,   John Jamison.

November ye	20,		David Sheerer.
	21,		Thomas Patton.
December ye	27,	1777.	Nicloss Whitsal.
	27,		John Willy.
March ye	24,	1778.	Frederick Dumbal.
	24,		Mathias Stokbergur.
Aprile ye	23,	1778.	George Huber.
	23,		Micham McHendry.
	25,		John Fiskey.
	25,		Christopher Reiner.
May ye	9,	1778.	Richard Young.
	13,		John Millar.
	16,		John Davis.
	16,		James Gher.
	25,		William Lochery.
	27,		Robert Fleeman.
	27,		James Willson.
	29,		James Steel.
	29,		Samuel Luis.
June ye	2,	1778.	George Ryan.
	2,		John Beck.
	19,		Garet Fiskey.
	19,		George Stokberger.
	19,		Joseph Craford.
	21,		John Pershon.
	21,		Jacob Lydich.
July ye	3,	1778.	James Parr.
	7,		Robert Marshall.
	7,		John McHee.
	23,		Arthur O'Horow.
	30,		Thomas Winter.
August	19,	1778.	William Waddle.
	29,		Peter Gross.
	31,		Daniel Armal.
September ye	9,	1778.	Benjamin Eakin.
	11,		James Cliford.
	21,		Jacob Powers.
October	9,	1778.	Marmaduke Jamison.
	12,		Abraham Powers.
	13,		John Telor.
	30,		Casper Weaver.
December	26,	1778.	George Findley.
	29,		Hendry Bair.
January ye	1,	1779.	John Beer.
	2,		John McEracin.
	4,		John Neele.

January ye 5,   George Orr.
         5,   Edmond Cochel.
         5,   Joseph Hussburne.
         5,   Samuel Glasgow.
         5,   James Egneu.
         5,   George Swap.
         5,   Charles Johnston.
         5,   Nathaniel Millar.

Ninety-Four in Number.

Westmoreland County:

I do certify the within account of 94 persons, having taken and subscribed the Oath of Allegiance before Hugh Martin, is recorded according to law.

JAMES KINKEAD, *Recorder.*

I (the subscriber hereof) do solemnly and sincerely declare and swear (or affirm) that the State of Pennsylvania is and of right ought to be a free, sovereign and Independent State. And I do forever renounce and refuse all allegiance, subjection and obedience to the king or crown of Great Britain; and I do further swear (or solemnly, sincerely and truly declare and affirm) that I never have since the Declaration of Independence, directly or indirectly, aided, assisted, abetted or in any wise countenanced the King of Great Britain, his generals, fleets, armies or their adherents in their claims upon these United States, and that I have ever since the Declaration of Independence thereof demeaned myself as a faithful citizen and subject to this or some one of the United States, and that I will at all times maintain and support the freedom, sovereignty, and independence thereof, so help you God.

December 8, 1778.

James Young, Esq.

December 11.

John F. Mifflin, Esq.,   Andrew Parker.
Peter Scull, Esq.,

December 12.

William Masters.

December 15.

John Camm,   James Hunter.

December 16.

Moses Archer,   Moses Gometz,
Swerin Erichson,   Jno. Christian Wagner.
Ephraim Evans,

December 18.

George Tirnes,   George Leib,
George Moore,   Jacob Nonoter,
Jacob Young,   William Meng,
George Young,   Philip Fullan.

December 22.

Samuel Wilcox,   James Blain.

December 23.

Philip Benezet,   Jno. Delworth.
William Morris,

December 24.

James Bostick,   Thomas Tufst.

December 26.

Presley Blackiston.

TO PENNSYLVANIA.

December 28.

David Clark,

George McGee,

Francis Eskillion,

Paul Fooks.

December 29.

Joseph Ferree.

December 31.

John Groves.

January 4, 1779.

Thomas Franklin.

January 5.

Samuel Howell.

January 6.

Josiah Matlock.

January 14.

William Crispin, Esq.

January 16.

John Howard,

John Wood,

Samuel C. **Morris**,

Thomas **Morris**.

January 18.

Robert Duncan.

January 26.

Samuel Starret, Esq.

January 28.

Charles Young,

James **Worrell**.

January 29.

George Kelly.

February 15.

Joseph H. Ellis.

February 16.

John Reedle.

February 18.

Matthew Pratt.

February 23.

John Andrew Mesersmith,

Michael Croll, **Esq.**

March 2.

Isaac Snowden.

March 12.

Jacob Fuller.

March 13.

Lewis Reese,

March 23.

William Ball,

William **Adcock**.

March 27.

Samuel Morris, Esq.,
Captain John Redman, Jr.,
Conrad Steger,

Israel Davis,
John Thomas.

March 29.

John Fowler,
John Sheppard,

Alexander Anderson,
Absolem Johnston.

March 30.

John Holmes,

Col. Lewis Nichola.

April 1.

Edward Biddle, Esq.,
Benjamin Thornton,
Ezekiel Story,
Nathan Boys,
Isaac Roach, Esq.,
Stephen Beasly,

Nicholas Fitzsimons,
John Reynolds,
George Meyers,
Joseph Quality,
George Garland, Esq.

April 5.

John Thornhill.

April 13.

Frederick Scholl,
George Goodman,

Griffith Owen.

May 3.

Lewis Joseph Dornu, of Germany.

May 10.

Frederick Dominick.

May 11.

Thomas Moore.

May 13.

William Rush, Esq.

May 19.

William Stevens.

May 24.

Martin Dehart.

May 25.

James Fudge

May 31.

Nathaniel Browne.

June 2.

Thomas Mullen,
Francis Kroasen,

John Hood, merch.

June 3.

Christopher Cave,

John Langstea.

June 4.

Eleazor Judah.

TO PENNSYLVANIA.

June 10.

Charles Pryor.

June 12.

Philip Kensey,
James Fletcher,

    Dennis Clark.

June 14.

David Clark.

July 9.

John Dowdney,

    Dean Jones.

July 10.

Samuel Young.

July 12.

Joseph Vandike,

    William Broades.

July 13.

John Tyson,

    Farrell Wade.

July 16.

Peter Fennemore.

July 17.

Jacob Netsell.

July 19.

Barnabas McShane.

July 20.

Samuel Hodgson,

    James Ham.

July 23.

Benjamin Seixas.

July 24.

William Leech.

July 26.

Edward Fitzrandolph,

    Martin Gillman.

July 27.

Benjamin Woods.

July 28.

George Thompson,

    Matthew Duncan.

July 30.

Pelatiah Webster,
Charles Seitz,
Joseph Spencer,
Doctor James Fallon,
John Vannost,
Francis Proctor, **Sr.**,
John Lyons,

    Lewis Taylor,
    John Levins,
    Richard Collier,
    Gilbert King,
    William Stevens,
    William Shute.

July 31.

John Hansminger,　　　　Samuel Hudson.
Charles Stowe,

August 1.

John Fustain,　　　　　Peter Whiteside.
George Spafford,

August 2.

William McDowell,　　　　Samuel Leaman,
Evan Evans,　　　　　　John Goodman,
Nathaniel Cranch,　　　　Mathias Roush,
William Webb,　　　　　Michael Owner,
Peter Rain,　　　　　　John Flahavan,
Humphrey Donohoe,　　　Christ. Irwine,
Philip Soust,　　　　　Thomas Irwine,
George Streton,　　　　Christopher Shultz,
John Long,　　　　　　James Tempest,
Michael Zeiner,　　　　John Head, baker,
Thomas Bidle,　　　　　William Gordon,
Edward McDermott,　　　William Paul,
Jacob Dimond,　　　　　William Berriman,
William Moore,　　　　Col. John Cadwallader,
Michael Rien,　　　　　Thomas Peters.
John Reinhard,

August 3.

Joseph Wharton.

August 7.

Thomas Davis.

August 9.

James Arthur.

August 11.

John McCarthy.

August 12.

James McCobb.

August 14.
　　　　　　　　　　John Stonemetz.

Bartholemi Tardiveau,
Pierre Tardiveau,

August 17.
　　　　　　　　　　George Conser.

Joseph Lynn,

August 19.

John Deighton

August 28.

John Longford,　　　　Michael Durney.

August 30.

Charles Shilback.

September 9.

Robert Aiken.

September 10.

David Jemmison, Jr.

September 15.

Will Cunningham.

September 20.

Joseph Bensson.

September 24.

James Byrne,
John Smallman,
John Stille,

George Arndt,
Alexander Tod,
Joseph Graysbury.

September 27.

John Knorr,
Patrick Byrne,

Doctor Thomas Bond.

September 28.

James Louis Fallaize.

September 29.

Lewis Keller,
Jacob Geiger,

Jacob Souder,
Joseph Fox, gentleman.

October 2.

William Beavan.

October 6.

James Gallagher,

William Moore Smith, **Esq.**

October 7.

Lewis Micke,
Joseph Shober,
James Ham, Jr.,

Nathan Cook,
Peter Henderson,
Staats Lawrence.

October 8.

William Chancellor,
Joseph Fox, Jr.,

Conrad Gerhard,
Joseph Sims.

October 9.

John Dowers.

October 11.

George Gosner,
Joseph Turner, Jr.,
Jonathan Penrose,
John McShane,
Robert Hogg,

Joseph Stamper,
Reynold Kean,
John Miller,
Garrett Cottinger.

October 12.

William Condy,
William Powell.

Chamless Allen,
Charles Keesler.

October 13.

Joseph Turner,
Philip Ling,
Patrick Hogan,
Tomas Hahanan,
Wm. Shaw,

James Conchy,
James Craig,
James Scott,
Timothy Carroll.

October 14.

Henry Lalor,
Benjamin Myers,

John Fries,
Thomas Barry.

October 15.

Philip Moynagh,
John O'Hara,
Joseph Harrison,
Matthias Harrison,

John Carrell,
Anthony Yeldall,
Jacob Spicer,
Jacob Bristol.

October 16.

Dennis Dougherty,
Michael Bower,

John Magee.

October 17

Doct. Richard Farmer.

October 18.

Jacob Mayer,
Joseph Traxeller,
Jeremiah Traxeller,
George Horne,
Thomas Parker,
Robert Cocks,
Samuel Jones,
David Bowen,
Joseph Standsbury,
James Sparks,
Peter Miller,
David Frankes,
Daniel Benezet, Jr.,
Peter Renandet Chevalier,
Bryan O'Harra,
Richard Tittermary,

James Culbertson,
Assheton Humphreys,
Samuel Jefferys,
Samuel Murdock,
Christopher Harberger,
Paul Beck,
John David Seckel,
Aneas Urgehart,
Charles Cook,
George Justice, Jr.,
Israel Hollowell,
Edward Home.
William Turner,
Richard Footman,
Thomas West,
Levi Hollingsworth.

October 19.

Thomas McFee,
Matthew McFee,
Samuel Jackson,
John Grover,
Paul Keller,
Zacharias Long,
Gasper Guyger,

Isaac Lort,
Thomas Coats,
John Morris,
Elias Botner.
James Cochran,
Jonathan Meredith,
Nicholas Brooks,

Richard Rundle,
Curtis Clay,
John Nicholson,
Robert Barr,
John Taylor,
Joseph Swift,
Lawrence Sickle,
Thomas Murgatroyd,
Henry White, physick,
Ezekiel Bull,
Thomas Hemphill,
William Fisher, Jr.,
John Potts, Jr.,
Thomas Cloredge,
Jehue Lloyd,

Benjamin Coats,
Joseph Engle,
Mordecai Lawrence,
Thomas Fitzgerald,
Edward Bartholomew,
Gerald Forrister,
Edward Cutbush,
John Alexander,
Peter Marot,
Patrick McGennis,
Matthew McHugh,
Thomas Canby,
Jno. Foulke,
Peter Simonson.

October 20.

Philip Super,
William Hill,
Thomas Bristol,
Charles Vanderen,
Silas Engle,
John Shaw,
John Lloyd,
George Snider,
John Cummings,
Cadwallader Morris,
William Hamilton,
John Bently,
Joseph Donaldson,
Matthew Clarkson, Jr.,
William Streckland,

Joseph Stride,
Andrew Thompson,
Samuel Britton,
Richard Renshaw,
Benjamin Mifflin, Jr.,
John Remond,
John Baptist Lemorre,
Joy Castle,
Joseph Perkin,
Abraham Comron,
Walter McAlpine,
David Hill,
William McCollogh,
Robert Longhead.

June 9.

Michael Ryan, Major in the Pennsylvania.

June 12.

Burtle Shee, Lieut. Col. and D. Q. M. G.

June 17.

George Painter, come of age of 18 years.

June 22.

Thomas Chappel, come of age 21 February, 1780.

July 5.

John Heard, taken the oath in Maryland.

October 10, 1780.

William Palmer, Cap. in Ct. Pallasky Legeon.
James Stevenson, Comiss. of Acct., East Departm't.

February 22, 1781.

Matthew McConnell.

March 9.

Sam'l Wharton, late of France.

June 14.

Matthew Mease, late from France.

October 9.

William Bingham, late from France,
Philip Snyder, Ensign in the 6 Penna. Reg.
Francis Nichols, late Lieut. Col. Pennsylv'a line.
William McCurdy,
Andrew Walker,
Lewellyn Davis, Lt. 5 Reg.,
Michael Harvey,
William Adams,
Francis Proctor, Jr.,
Alexander Stewart, Surgeon 3rd Pennsylvania Reg.,
William Murren,
Job Vernon, Cap. 5 Penna. Regt.
Levi Griffith,
Wm. W. Smith,
Thomas Forrest,
Alexander Anderson,
James McCulloch,
Benj. Perry,
David Zeigler,
J. Grier,

E. Crawford,
John Lucas,
John Craig,
George Bush,
W. Wilson.
Joseph Howell, Jr., Aud'r Acct. Cl. Army.
Matthias Sadler,
William Craig, 3rd Pennsy'a Reg., Cap.,
Edw'd F. Randolph, Lieut. 4th Penn. Regt.,
Harman Stouts, Cap. 10 Penna. Regem't,
Dan'l Smith, of Cape May,
Worsley Emes,
Robert Coltman,
Jas. Ashton, Lt. Penn'a Artt'y,
Corn's McKaskey, late Ass't Commss'r of F——,
John Downey,
John Slay,
Joseph Slay,
William Bills.

I do (the subscriber hereof) solemnly swear (or affirm) that I renounce and refuse all allegiance to George the Third King of Great Britain, his heirs and successors, and that I will be faithful and bear true allegiance to the Commonwealth of Pennsylvania as a free and independent State, and that I will not at any time hereafter do or cause to be done any matter or thing that will be prejudicial or injurious to the freedom and independence thereof, as declared by Congress. And also that I will discover and make known, to some one Justice of the Peace of the said State, all treasons and traitorous conspiracies, which I know, or hereafter shall know, to be formed against this or any of the United States of America.

A list of the names of Strangers that have taken the above oath agreeable to act of Assembly, 5th December, 1778:

Dec. 11, 1778. Henry Osbourne, Attorney-at-Law.

Jan. 25, Philip Francis, from West Florida.

Jared Ingersell, Esqr., lately from France.

June, 9, John McDougal, late of Jamaica.

Jan. 12, 1780. Nathaniel Houghton, from France.

13, George Haynes, from St .Eustatia, Merchant.

Mar. 7, John Templeman, late from London.

June 9, John Leamy, from Spain, Merchant.

John Sharp, from Spain, Merchant.

William Sharp, from Spain, Merchant.

30, Gullam Abertson, Junr., from St Eustatia, Merchant.

Dec. 8, Joseph Willson, from Ireland, Merchant.

11, John Ross, lately from France.

John Crag, lately from St. Eustatia.

Jan. 1, 1781. James Hamilton, from Ireland.

July 14, Wm. Barclay, from Ireland.

23, Thomas Hutchens, Geographer of the United States.

27, George Hughes, from Ireland, by way of Statia.

Oct. 2, Peter Adrain, from France.

5, Michael Morgan O'Brien, from Martinico.

Oct. 9, 1781. Patrick Moore, from Martinico.

William Bingham.

Nov. 30, 1778. Christopher Meyers, late of the West Indies.

No. 1.

October 12, 1784. Henry Land.

Ab. Jones.

Janthena Chtteinken.

Antoine Joseph Fillet.

October	12, 1784.	Samuel House.
		Robert Crozer.
	15,	Stephen Burrowes,
		John Campbell,
		Minsarl Taurer,
		His
		Martin ✕ Kinsel.
		mark.
		Jno. Steele.
		William Kunckel.
		Jon'n Burraii.
		Alex'r Foster.
		Th. R. Kennedy.
November	3,	Samuel Kearney.
	24,	John Maag.
		Jacob Hayman.
		And'w Jamison.
January	20, 1785.	Tobias Jacob.
February	11,	Herman J. Lambaert.
March	10,	Robert Davis.
May	23,	Goetan Perrogalli.
	28,	Garrett Willson.
		Lawrence Toomy.
	31,	Thomas Connell.
June	2,	Jno. Thompson.
	3,	Dan'l Stephens.
	4,	Samuel Davis Greene.
	18,	James Fraizor.
	25,	Rich'd Nowland.
		Jerry Myles.
July	9,	John McCarter.
	15,	Samuel Noah.
	28,	Samuel Merrian.
	30,	Joseph B. McKean.
		His
September	26, 1785.	John ✕ Jacobs.
		mark.
	30,	Benj'n Mason.

The foregoing is a true list of the persons who have taken the Oaths of Allegiance since the 10th of last October, 1784, up to this 1st of October, 1785, before

WILL ADCOCK. [SEAL.]

Inrolled, 20 October, 1790.

No. 2.

Philadelphia County, ss:

I do hereby certify unto Mathew Irwin, Esquire, Recorder of Deeds for the county aforesaid, that the following persons have severally taken the Oath, or Affirmation, of Fidelity and Allegiance unto the State of Pennsylvania, before me, the subscriber one of the Justices of the Peace in and for the county aforesaid, agreeable to the Act of General Assembly passed the 13th day of June, 1777, viz:

Bartholomew Archibold,	David Malin,
Alexander Plunkett,	John Malin,
James Ross,	Henry Miller,
Thomas Dixey,	Henry Hoffner
James Loug,	

October the 11th. 1785.

SAM'L WHARTON.

Inrolled. 20 October, 1790.

No. 3.

Philadelphia County, ss:

I do hereby certify that unto Mathew Irwin, Esquire, Recorder of Deeds for the county aforesaid, that the following persons have severally taken the Oath, or Affirmation, of Fidelity and Allegiance unto the State of Pennsylvania, before me, the subscriber, one of the Justices of the Peace in and for the county aforesaid, as prescribed in and by the act of General Assembly, passed the 5th day of December, 1778, viz:

Martin Barry,	John Marton,
John Bunting,	James Sclatten,
Benjamin Bunting,	Michael Burke, lately arrived
William Maulsby,	from Ireland.
Hamilton Hazleton,	

October the 11th, 1785.

SAM'L WHARTON.

Inrolled, 20 October, 1790.

No. 4.

List of persons who have taken the Oath of Allegiance to the Commonwealth of Pennsylvania since the 7th of October, 1784, before me, the subscriber:

Dec. 1, 1784. John Leacock Hill, from London.

Feb. 22. 1785. George Chaplain, of Lombard street, Philada.

25, John Robertson.

Sept. 7, John Crawford, from Ireland, who has been arrived here, *i. e.,* in this State two years.

16, John Smith Lister.

26, Alexander Philips, from London, Taylor; he arrived here and settled in and near the city of Philadelphia more than one year.

Given under my hand and seal the 1st of October, 1785.

SAM'L WHARTON, [SEAL.]

Inrolled, 20 October, 1790.

No. 5.

OCTOBER 5, 1787.

Sir: The following persons have made oath before me, agreeable to act of Assembly passed the 4th day of March, 1786, respecting allegiance and fidelity.

I am, sir, y'r most h'ble servant,

SAM'L WHARTON.

Oct.   7,   1786. Norman × McCally, Labourer,   in Shippen
His   mark.

street, district of Southwark, county of Philadelphia.

10,   James Gamble, Second street, district of Southwark, in the county of Philadelphia.

Mark Collins, captain of a sea vessel, district of Southwark, in the above county.

Inrolled. 20 October, 1790.

No. 6.

Record of persons' names who have taken and subscribed the following oath of allegiance and fidelity before Jonathan Penrose, Esq., agreeably to an act of Assembly passed the fourth day March, one thousand seven hundred and eighty-six, viz:

We do swear (or solemnly, sincerely and truly declare and affirm) that we renounce and refuse all allegiance to George the Third, King of Great Britain, his heirs and successors; and that we will be faithful and bear true allegiance to the Commonwealth of Pennsylvania, as a free and independent State; and that we will not, at any time, do or cause to be done any matter or thing that will be prejudicial or injurious to the freedom and independence thereof; and we do further swear (or solemnly, sincerely and truly declare and affirm) that we never have, since the Declaration of the Independence of the United States of America, voluntarily joined, aided, assisted or abetted the King of Great Britain, his generals, fleets or armies, or their adherents (knowing them to be such) whilst employed against the said United States, or either of them.

District of Southwark.

March	22, 1786.	affirmed,	Joseph Bird.
		oath,	Samuel Muschell.
		oath,	John Cavan.
		oath,	George McKegg.
		oath,	William Hubbard,
		oath,	Charles Smith,
		oath,	James Irvin,
		oath,	William Kemp.
April	3,	affirmed,	Joseph Williamson.
	19,	oath,	Peter Young.
May	8,	oath,	William Gamble.
		oath,	John Gamble.
July	22,	oath,	Francis Moore.
Sept.	6,	oath,	John Edgworth.
	27,	oath,	Ebenezer Call.
	30,	affirmed,	John Bissell.

JON'N PENROSE. [SÉAL.]

Inrolled, 20 October, 1790.

No. 7.

A list of persons who have taken the test to the State of Pennsylvania before me:

September 8, 1785.

William Buckley.

September 26.

Michael Waltman.

Israel Morris,
John Foulke,

October 10.

James Cox,
John Padmore,
Charles Cox.
Henry Cook,

Nicholas Avory,
Edward Ward,
Jeremiah Satchwell,
Wm. Walter Humphreys,

James Sawyer,
George McKay,
John Beale,
James Smith,
Ezekial Yarnall,
Joseph Sargeant,
Richard Dale,
William Anderson,
Isaac Wainwright,
John Saunders,
Joseph Potts, Junr.,
David Rutter,
John Stillwell,
Richard Stiles,
John Hart,
William Taylor,
Owen Waters,
John Karr,
Andrew Young,

John Gregory,
John Webber,
Alexander Fayerweather,
John Keiser,
Richard Sparks,
Joseph Allen, Junr.,
David Simpson,
John Witherup,
Nathaniel Lewis,
Neill Matheson,
Thomas Finley,
John Gillmore,
John Bennett,
James Ince,
Mathew M. Clarkson,
William Campble,
Jonathan Wainwright,
Owen McGlocklin,
John Battin.
Benj'n Crawford,
Elisha Crowell,
Richard Samson,
John Anselmo Douin de la
   Combe,
Thomas Emerson,

Hugh Newbigging,
John McGreggor,
Thomas Ackley,
Anthony Dowland,
Thomas Dixey,
John Hoy,
Joseph Poole,
Thomas Napier,
Robert Taylor,
John Cox,
Henry Manly,
Michael Allen,
Edmund McKensey,
John Gass,
Frederick Myers,
George Griffin,
James Musgrave,
Thomas Willson,
Arthur Donaldson.

October 11.

John Marshall,
Joseph Williams,
John Robinson,
William Donner,
John McPhail,
William McPhail,
Alexander McPhail,
Bartholomew Baker,
John Bell,
Philip Fish.
William Hulbert,
Lewis Runer,
William McIlroy,
Daniel Mullen,
Samuel Adam,
Jacob Lipp,
George Bigler,
John Chester,
Samuel Crawford,
Thomas McBride,
John Poyntell,
Michael O'Brian,

James Stewart.

November 14, 1785. James Story.
      23,   Joseph Heaverill.
December 5,   William Baird.
      19,   John Mitchell.
      26,   John McMinn.
January 28, 1786. Joseph Muhler.
      7,   Hans Cordland.
      11,   William Flick.
October 6,   Evan Truman.
      7,   Joseph Shoemaker.
                Benjamin Jones.
                John Thompson.
      9,   Robert Wharton.
                Thomas Baker.
      7,   Campble Dick.
                Thomas Hood.
                William Long.
      10,   John Slaughter.
                Samuel Johnston.
                Daniel Smith.
      2,   Charles Carlvon.
                William Lee.
      9,   Lawrence Carrol.

N. B.—The following should have been inserted before:

March 3, 1786.

Robert Allen,	John McCollom,
Samuel Gernish,	Norton Pryor, Jr.,
William Johnston,	Benjamin Evans,
George Bartram,	George Cantlers,
Bonsall James,	James Stewart,
Henry Beam,	William Pattin,
Andrew Nonamaker,	Westor Clark,
Christopher Irick,	Daniel Haler.
James Austin,	

April 6.

William Sykes,	John Cowan,
James Patten,	Francis Smith,
John King,	William English,
Patrick Bradley,	Toly Park,

April 7.

Archibald Carr.

SIR:—Whatever the law allows me to pay on the above list
(within the time) shall be paid by, sir,
          Your ob. h'ble serv't,

                        JO. WHARTON.

Math'w Erwine, Esqr.
Inrolled the 20th October, 1790.
   4—VOL. III.

No. 8.

The following list of persons who have taken the test likewise produced by Joseph Wharton:

October 10, 1786.

Thomas Ames,
John McCormack,
John Heeny,
Charles Harris,
Robert Ray,
Joseph Behringer,
Thomas Anderson,
Abraham Hubbard,
Jacob Wesby,
Benjamin Thomas,
David Harding,

John Miller, Junr.,
Lawrence Kelly,
John Somers,
Lawrence Allwine,
Nathaniel Keane,
Thomas Wetherill,
Samuel Carver,
John Fisher,
Charles Callahan,
William Ashby,
James Dunlap,

April 12.

John Smith.

October 10.

George Marvine,
Joseph Good,

Robert Williams.

December 18.

Robert McFall.

February 27, 1787.

Gustavus Cuningham, renewed.

August 24.

James Enew.

September 22.

Thomas Parr Wharton.

October 6.

Richard Babe,
John Somerville,

James Hazlet,
John Menzes.

October 8.

John Breintnall Ackley,

David Lewis.

October 9.

Alexander Harvey.

October 10.

Thomas Stanes,

Joseph Ashbridge.

November 15.

John Christy, Mariner.

December 3.

James Kelhcher, Mariner.

December 5.

John Reily.

December 10.

Francis Jack.

PHILADELPHIA, *December* 11, 1789. A true copy delivered to Mathew Erwin, Esqr., Recorder of Deeds, &c.

JO. WHARTON.

Inrolled, 20th October, 1790.

No. 9.

A list of the names of persons who took the Oath, or affirmation of Allegiance to this State, passed the fourth of March, 1786:

Mar.	15,	Absalem Michener, of Bristol township, Philadelphia county, Farmer.
		Jacob Lukens, of Bristol township, Miller.
		John Cochran, of this City.
	18,	Christopher Rapp, of Bristol township, Philadelphia county, Farmer.
	21,	James C. Fisher, of Philadelphia, Merchant.
		Benjamin Gibb, of Philadelphia.
April	5,	Peter Beck, of this city, Cordwainer.
May	6,	John Stedot, of this city, Tavernkeeper.
June	6,	Robert Worrell, Blacksmith, Oxford township, Philadelphia county.
Sept	27,	Isaiah Worrell, of ditto, Shopkeeper.
Oct	5,	David Lauck, of this city, Cooper.
	7,	William West, North'n Liberties, Gent'n.
	9,	Charles Wilstach, of this city, Shopkeeper.
		John Hallman, of this city, Cordwainer.
	10,	John Case, of the North'n Liberties, Taylor.
		Jacob Krener, of this city, Cordwainer.
		George Teace, of this city, Tobacconist.
		Alexander Willson, of the North'n L., Tanner.
		Sante Steverong, of this city, Porter.
		John Barnes, of ditto, Hatter.
		James Wallace, of ditto, butcher.
		John George Mayer, ditto, Baker.
		Abraham Dull, ditto, House Carpenter.
		Abraham Hartman, do., Laborer.
		John Michael Barth, ditto, Taylor.
Oct.	10,	Joseph Warner, Jr. do., Boat Builder.
		Christopher White, do., Porter.
		Philip Reaver, do., Breeches Maker.
		Henry Hildebrand, ditto, House Carpenter.

Oct.   10.   George Einwachter, Labourer.
                Joseph Leyendecker, ditto.
                John Wright, N. Liberties, Barber.
                Frederick Anthony, ditto, Labourer.
                Frederick Winkle, ditto, ditto.
                Marden Cost, N. Liberties, Laborer.
                Joseph Pepper, ditto, Carter.
                Charles Conrad, of the N. Liberties, **Labourer.**
                Nathan Marple, of this city, Labourer.
                Mathias Champ, ditto, Labourer.
                Leonard Ron, ditto, Carter.
                Conrad Bachman, ditto, Taylor.
                John Kever, of this city, Cordwainer.
                Henry Soust, ditto, Tallow Chandler.
                James Cornish, ditto, Turner.
                Jacob Endress, of the N. Liberties, **Carter.**
                Edward Shandzey, of this city, Labourer.
                William Higgins, of the North Liber., ditto.
                Elisha Crosby, of this city, Hatter.
                Andrew Haney, of this city, Hatter.
                Abraham Hatter, ditto. Blacksmith.
                Jacob Baker, ditto, ditto.
                Andrew Martin, ditto, Labourer.
                William Kinnard, ditto, House Carpenter.
                Darby Dohana, ditto, ditto.
                Alexander McKinley, ditto.
April   14, 1787. George Ewart, of this city, Gentleman.
        21,   John Salter, Jr., ditto, Baker.

{ SEAL } Witness my hand and seal September 24th, 1787.
                                WILLIAM RUSH,

Inrolled the 20th October, 1790.

No. 10.

A list of persons who have taken the test according to a law
past the fourth day of March 1786 for taking the test.

                        ISAAC HOWELL, *North Ward.*

Mar.   9. 1776. Jacob Downing, Merchant, affirmed.
        13,   Samuel Harper, Blacksmith, affirmed.
        15,   Richard Tunis, Lower Merion, Farmer, affirmed.
        20,   Joseph Walker, Grocer, affirmed.
        21,   Benj. Pennington, Gentleman, affirmed.
                John Lipp, Taylor, affirmed.
        25,   John Leech, Sen'r, Blockly, sworn.
April   3.   John Singer, Trader, sworn.
        8,   Joseph Rakestraw, Carpent., affirmed.

April	10,	William Roberts, Carpent., sworn.
	17,	Burton Wallace, Bricklayer, sworn.
	18,	Philip Price, of Kingsessing, affirmed.
	24,	Michael Dennison, innkeeper, affirmed.
May	8,	Daniel Clangs, Painter, sworn.
		James Worstall, Storekeeper, affirmed.

—— Gorman, } forenoon, sworn,
Chevalier Chaderac, }

	13,	John Lownes, Gentleman, affirmed.
	22,	George Davis, Gentleman, sworn.
Sept.	23,	Peter Waggoner, Cordwainer, sworn.
	29,	John Stephens, Sadler, sworn.
Oct.	3.	Melcher Wissinger, Wier Worker, sworn.
		George Merkely, Cordwainer, affirmed.
		Joseph Watson, Cordwainer, affirmed.
		Benjamin Oldden, Cordwainer, affirmed.
	6,	George Ashton, Merchant, affirmed.
		Abraham Bickley, Merchant, sworn.
	7,	Enock Richardson, Carpenter, sworn.
		Peter Bockeus, Ropemaker, sworn.
		Christopher Henry Sanderman, sworn.
		John P. De Haas, Merchant.
		Brightwell Hibbs. Taylor, affirmed.
		John Rubb, Merchant, sworn.
Oct.	9, 1786.	Israel Paxon, Currier, affirmed.
		John Jones, Currier, sworn.
		Mathew Conrad, Innkeeper, affirmed.
Oct.	10, 1786.	Robert Hiltzheimer, Merchant, sworn.
		Samuel Shoemaker, Carpenter, sworn.
		James Littlejohn, Cordwainer. sworn.
		Robert Shoemaker, Carpenter, affirmed.
		John Chew Thomas, Student-at-law, affirmed.
		Godfrey Rarich, tobacconist, sworn.
		Samuel Howell, Brushmaker. affirmed.
		John Lindemer, Chairmaker, sworn.
		Jesse Care, Saddle-tree maker, affirmed.
		Philip Edenburn, Trader, sworn.
		John Grandom, Merchant, affirmed.

His
John × Perkerson. Labor., sworn.
mark.

Elisha Fisher, Clark, affirmed.
John Gill, Cordwainer, affirmed.
William Weaser, Carpenter, sworn.
Nehemiah Sharp, Taylor, affirmed.
George Hamble, Cordwainer, affirmed.
John Johnson, Hatter, sworn.

Oct.   10, 1786. Garret Hewes, Cordwainer, affirmed.
                   Thomas Tiplen, ditto, sworn.
                   Andrew Ealy, Farmer, ditto.
                   John Conrad, Blacksmith, affirmed.
                   James Chatters, Cordwainer, sworn.
                   Samuel Porter, Taylor, sworn.
                   Jacob Friss, Farmer, sworn.
                   Jacob Tibley, Wheelwright, sworn.
                   James S. Dougherty, Harnis, sworn.
                   Job Hatheway, Carpenter, ditto.
                   Abraham Wynkoop, Coachmaker, ditto.
                   Daniel Bochius, ditto, ditto.
                   Jacob Allemus, ditto, ditto.
                   John Fisher, Harnessmaker, ditto.
                   George Carlisle, Coachmaker, ditto.
                   Joseph Mártin, House Carpenter, ditto.
                   James Lewis, Taylor, affirmed.
                   John Abel, Breeches Maker, sworn.
                   John Holberg, Limner, ditto.
                   Aaron Palmer, Hatter, affirmed.

Oct.   10, 1786. Henry Bowles, Baker, sworn.

Oct.   31,   John Hung, Shopkeeper, do.

April   12, 1787. Frederick de Montmollein, Merch't, sworn.

                                   ISAAC HOWELL.

Inrolled the 20th October, 1790.

No. 11.

List of the names and surnames of those who have given test of allegiance to this State, agreeable to the act passed the 4th March, 1786, before me.

                                 PLUNK'T FLEESON.

March   9, 1786. John Todd, Schoolmaster, of Philad'a.
                   John Eldridge, Shopkeeper, do.
                   Samuel Jones, House Carpenter, do.
                   Samuel Bettle, Taylor, do.
                   John Burchall, Shoemaker, do.

           16,   Jacob Teasel, Grocer, do.

April   7,   John Clark, Silk Dier, do.

           13,   Thomas Howard, Watchmaker, do.

May   8,   Thomas Appleby, Distiller, do.
                   Joseph Rebaud, Shopkeeper, do.

Aug.   23,   Jeremiah Cresson, Gentleman, do.

Oct.   5,   Samuel Bringhurst, do.

            7,   George Steel, Shoemaker, late of **Delaware** State.

Oct.   7.   James Mease, Schoolmaster of Philadelphia, do.

    10,   Samuel Davis, Merch't. do.
    Henry Brosias, Taylor, do.
    James Preston, Cordwainer, do.
    John Souder, Mariner. do.
    Barney Mier, Soapboiler, do.
    James Sutton, Carpenter, do.
    Richard Thompson, Inspector of Tobacco, do.
    William Lloyd, House Carpenter, do.
    James Batton, Labourer, do.
    Jacob Grace, Labourer, do.

Oct.   10, 1786. James Ord, Labourer, of Philad'a, do.
    Samuel Hall, do., do.
    William Drake, do., do.

Nov.   16, 1786. John Colleral Frosh, a native of New York, Mariner.

May   9, 1787. Henry Lentz.

    Taken agreeably to the act of 29th March, 1787:

Sept.   20, 1787. William Gibbs, lately from France, a native of Boston.
    Peter Benj'n Audebert, Merch't, resident in this city above two years.
    Alexander Freeman, Coachmaker, resident in the city above two years.
    Daniel DeBray, Merch't, resident in this city above 37 years.

    Copy from my register to October 1st, 1787.

                PLUNK'T FLEESON.

    Inrolled the 20th October, 1790.

No. 12.

A list of persons who have given test of allegiance to this State since this date, before Plunket Fleeson, to October 14, 1788:

Oct.   4, 1787. Daniel Bray, Merchant, arrived in this city three years past.

    8,   George Reinhart, Junior, Coach Painter, Fourth Street.
    Wolffgang Metoch, of South ward, Winecoper.
    John Greer, of Middle ward, Dealer.

    9,   Samuel Falwell, of Philadelphia, Painter.
    David Lukens, of same. Coachmaker.
    Henry Weaver, of same, Merchant.
    Isaac Johnson, of same, Shoemaker.
    Richard Carlton, of same, Taylor.

Oct.	9.	William Guier, of same, Grazier.
		William Garrick, of same, a Mariner.
		James Skerret, of same, Blacksmith.
		Andrew Murrey, of same, House Carpenter.
		James McClure, of same, Baker.
Nov.	6,	Richard Stockton, of same Gentleman.
		William Kinnear, of same, Blacksmith.
		Jacob Reese, of same, Merchant.
		Josiah Siddons, of same, Taylor.
		John Craven, of same, Clark.
		Richard Crean, of Blockley, Farmer.
		John Stoy, of Philadelphia, Taylor.
Dec.	13,	George Wallington, of same, a Mariner.
		John Wallington, of same, Scrivener.
Jan.	3, 1788.	Robert Haydock, of same, Plumer.
	9,	David Robinson, of same, Watchmaker.
	15,	Robert Hopkins, of Point-no-Point, N. Liberties.
Feb.	13,	Jacob Wiltberger, of Philadelphia, Currier.
		Joseph Wilds, of same, Bricklayer.
		Daniel Kings, Junr., of same, Brass Founder.
April	2,	William Wood, of same, Taylor and Shopkeeper.
	14,	William Dresky, of same, arrived from Amsterdam near 4 years past.
	26,	James Fleming, Weaver, from Ireland, arrived here above 3 years past.
May	15,	George Kemp, of Philadelphia, Writer.
Oct.	14,	William Reynolds, returned with ye list of this day.

PLUNK'T FLEESON.

Inrolled, 20th October, 1790.

No. 13.

City of Philadelphia, ss :

To Mathew Irwin, Esquire, Recorder of Deeds for the City and County of Philadelphia:

I do hereby certify that Augustino Domique Viand, Mariner, aged thirty years, born at Bordeaux, in the Province of Guienne, in the Kingdom of France, son of Daniel Viand, Merchant, of Bordeaux, and Mary, his wife, and who came last from Corunna, in Biscay, in the Kingdom of Spain, to this city, personally appeared before me, Samuel Powell, Esquire, Mayor of the said city, on the twenty-sixth day of September, in the year of our Lord one thousand seven hundred and eighty-nine, and voluntarily took and subscribed the Oath of Allegiance and Fidelity to the Commonwealth of Pennsylvania, conformably to an act of the General Assembly of the said Commonwealth, passed the thirteenth day of March, A. D. 1789. In testimony whereof I have hereunto set my hand and seal this thirtieth day of September, A. D. 1789.

SAMUEL POWELL, *Mayor*.

Inrolled, 20 October, 1790.

No. 14.

A list of persons who have taken and subscribed the oath of fidelity and allegiance to the Commonwealth of Pennsylvania, with time of taking and subscribing the oath, occupation, age, place of nativity, parents' names and occupations, and place from whence they came last:

October 23, 1789. Thomas, Lindsay, Yeoman, thirty-six, parish of Denistee, county of Cork, Ireland; Thomas Lindsay, Yeoman, and Mary his wife, London.

October 26. Thomas Scott, Mariner, forty-two, Air, Airshire, Scotland; Hugh Scott, Yeoman, of Air, and Marian Scott, Lisbon.

October 30. Roger Hamill, Mariner, twenty-eight, parish of Deriaghy, county of Antrim, Ireland; Daniel Hamill, Linnen Manufacturer, of said parish and county, and Issamiah, his wife, New York.

November 10. Robert Fox, Mariner, twenty-eight, parish of Kilmore, county of Cavan, Ireland; John Fox, Husbandman, and Jane, his wife, New York.

November 12. Matthew Martineaux, Merchant, thirty-four, Bordeaux, province of Guinne, France; Peter Martineaux, Merch't of Bordeau, and Martha, his wife, Cape Francois.

November 12. Thomas Lillibridge, Mariner, twenty-six, Newport, Rhode Island; Robert Lillibridge, Merch't, of Newport, Rhode Island, and Alice, his wife, Cape Francois.

November 14. Noel Quesnel, Merchant, thirty-eight, Dieppe, province of Normandy, France; Paul Quesnel, Merch't, of Dieppe, and Catherine, his wife, Haver de Grace.

October 20. Thomas Smith, mariner, thirty-six, parish of Workington, county of Cumberland, G. Britain; John Smith, of Workington, county of Cumberland, Great Britain, Mariner, and Jane, his wife, St. Ubes, Portugal.

December 2. Thomas Galgey, Mariner, thirty-four, city of Waterford, Ireland; Richard Galgey, of Waterford, Mariner, and Barbara, his wife, Kingston, Jamaica.

December 5. Amos Ireland, Mariner, twenty-nine, Philadelphia, Pennsylvania; Amos Ireland, Yoeman, of Philad'a, and Sarah, his wife, Lucca, Jamaica.

December 5. Christopher Lee, Mariner, twenty-three, Christiana in Norway; Christian Lee, Officer of the Customs, Christiana in Norway, and Olena, his wife, Cape Francois.

December 5. Peter Holliday, Mariner, twenty-one, White Haven, Gt. Britain; Edward Holliday, Linnen Draper, of White Haven, and Elizabeth, his wife, Domnique and Boston, New England.

December 5. Daniel Doyle, Mariner, twenty-three, Waterford city, Ireland; Dennis Doyle, officer in the customs at Waterford, and Sarah, his wife, Cadiz, in Spain.

December 5. Joseph Bartin, Mariner, twenty-eight, Leghorn, Dukedom of Tuscany; Francis Bartin, of Leghorn, Mariner, and Mary, his wife, Cape Francois.

December 5 John Smith, Mariner, twenty-two, Berwick upon Tweed; John Smith, Carpenter, of Berwick upon Tweed, and Mary, his wife, Bordeaux.

December 8. Edmund Nowlan, Mariner, thirty-four, county of Galway, Ireland; Terence Nowlan, Yoeman, of the county of Galway, and Catherine, his wife, Tobago.

December 8. Michael Ashmenall, Mariner, twenty-two, Southwold, Suffolk, England; John Ashmenall, Mariner, of Southwold, Suffolk, and Mary, his wife, Oporto.

December 8. John Lum, Mariner, twenty-two, Philadelphia, Pennsylvania; John Lum, Ship Carpenter, of Philadelphia, and Hannah, his wife, India.

December 8. Anthony Bodkin, Mariner, twenty-seven, Innislaken, county of Galway, Ireland; James Bodkin, Mariner, of Innislaken, county of Galway, Ireland, and Bibian, his wife, Turks Islands.

December 8. John Skinner, Mariner, twenty-four, Bristol, in England; John Skinner, of Bristol, Shoemaker, and Jane, his wife, Amsterdam.

December 8. John Crea, Mariner, twenty-four, Greenoch, in Scotland; John Crea, of Greenoch, House Carpenter, and Agnes Marcus, his wife, Amsterdam.

City of Philadelphia, ss: I do hereby certify that the persons whose names are inserted in the foregoing list have taken the oath of fidelity and allegiance to the Commonwealth of Pennsylvania before me, Samuel Powell, Esquire, Mayor of the said city. In testimony whereof I have hereunto set my hand and affixed my seal this tenth day of December, in the year of our

{ SEAL } Lord one thousand seven hundred and eighty-nine.

SAMUEL POWELL, *Mayor.*

Inrolled, 20th October, 1790.

No. 15.

A list of persons who have taken and subscribed the oath of fidelity and allegiance to the Commonwealth of Pennsylvania, time of taking and subscribing the oath, persons' names, occupation, age, place of nativity, parents' names and occupations, and place from whence they last came.

January 16, 1790. Peter Walsh, Merchant, thirty two, Waterford city, in Ireland; Walter Walsh, Merch't, of Waterford city, and Elizabeth, his wife, L'Orient to Boston.

February 1. Bernard Magee, Mariner, twenty-five, Turkish, in the county of Down, Ireland; Dennis Magee, of Turkish, in the county of Down, and Mary, his wife, Bombay to New York.

March 19. Michael Terman, Mariner, fifty, Catta, in the Republic of Venice; Antonia Terman, of Catta, Mariner, and Catherine, his wife, Cadiz.

March 20. Francis Clery Dupont, Yeoman, twenty-eight, Boulogne, in Picardy in France; Francis Dupont, of Boulogne, in Picardy in France, Merch't and Catherine Clery, his wife, Havre de Grace, in France.

City of Philadelphia, Pennsylvania, ss:

I do hereby certify that the foregoing is a true list of all the persons who have taken the Oath of Fidelity and Allegiance to the Commonwelth of Pennsylvania, since the last return made to the Recorder of Deeds for the city and county of Philadelphia, on the tenth day of December, in the year of our Lord one thousand seven hundred and eighty-nine.

Witness my hand and seal this sixth day of April, in the year of our Lord one thousand seven hundred and

{ SEAL }   ninety.

SAMUEL POWELL, *Mayor.*

Inrolled, 20th October, 1790.

No. 16.

Aug. 31, 1790. John Dunn, Mariner, 35. Princess Ann county, Virginia, James and Margaret Dunn, House Carpenter, county of Shelbourne, Nova Scotia.

City of Philadelphia, ss:

I do hereby certifie that the above is a true copy of all who have taken and subscribed the Oath of Allegiance and Fidelity to the Commonwealth of Pennsylvania, according to law, before me, the subscriber, one of the Aldermen, from the first of October 1789, to the first of October, 1790. Given under my hand and seal this first day of October, 1790.

REYNOLD KEEN.

No. 17.

I, Hilary Baker, one of the Aldermen of the city of Philadelphia, do hereby certify that the following is a true list of the persons who have, before, me, taken the Oath of Allegiance to the Commonwealth of Pennsylvania, as prescribed by act of Assembly, passed the thirteenth day of March, 1789, viz:

George Shea, Merchant, son of John Shea, of the city of Cork, in the Kingdom of Ireland, merchant, and of Mary, his wife, born in the city of Cork aforesaid, last arrived in the city of Philadelphia from the city of New York, took the Oath of Allegiance on the 25th day of December, 1789.

Francis Hamilton, Weaver, son of Francis Hamilton, farmer, and Jane, his wife, born in the parish of Magherally, in the county of Downe, in the Kindgom of Ireland, last arrived in this city from Wilmington, in the State of Delaware, took the Oath of Allegiance on the sixth day of March, 1790.

Jacob Philip Guilgot, Gentleman, son of Joseph Guilgot, gentleman, and Magdalen Lovinia, his wife, born at Epenel, in the Province of Lorraine, in the Kingdom of France, last arrived in this city from the city of New York, took the Oath of Allegiance on the seventeenth day of April, 1790.

James Kierman, Labourer, son of John Kierman, farmer, and Ann, his wife born in the Parish of Cill, in the county of Cavin, in the Kingdom of Ireland last arrived from the town of Waterford, in the Kingdom of Ireland, took the Oath of Allegiance on the 22d day of May, 1790.

{ SEAL {   In witness wheref I have hereunto set my hand and seal the first day of October, 1790.

                                     HILARY BAKER.

Inrolled, the 20th October, 1790.

John Collect, Mariner, son of Robert Collect, of the Isle of Man, in the Kingdom of Great Britain, blacksmith, and Ann his wife born in the Isle of Man, aged thirty-eight years, last from London, hath taken the Oath of Allegiance to the Commonwealth of Pennsylvania before Samuel Miles, Esquire. Mayor of the city of Philadelphia, on the 30th of April, 1790.

Timithy Organ, Mariner, son of Denis Organ, of Cork, in Ireland, rigger, and Mary, his wife, born in the city of Cork, aged twenty-five years, last from Norfolk, but now of the city of Philadelphia, hath taken the Oath of Allegiance to the Commonwealth of Pennsylvania before Samuel Miles, Mayor of the city of Philadelphia, on the first day of July, 1790.

Thomas Hornsby, son of Thomas Hornsby, of Alexandria, in the State of Virginia, mariner, and Mary, his wife, born in Alexandria, aged twenty-two years, last from Alexandria, but now of the city of Philadelphia, hath taken and subscribed the

Oath of Allegiance and Fidelity to the Commonwealth of Pennsylvania before Samuel Miles, Esquire, Mayor of the city of Philadelphia, on the sixth of July, A. D. 1790.

John Gifford, Mariner, son of Robert Gifford, of Danby, on North Waters, in Great Britain, and Mary his wife, born in Danby, aged Forty years, last from Baltimore, but now of the city of Philadelphia, hath taken and subscribed the Oath of Allegiance and Fidelity to the Commonwealth of Pennsylvania, before Samuel Miles, Esquire, Mayor of the City of Philadelphia, on the fourth day of August, Anno Domini 1790.

Jacob Giblett, Mariner, son of Hugh Giblett, of Clevedon, in the county of Somerset, in Great Britian, Husbandman, and Elizabeth, his wife, born in Clevedon, aged thirty-five years, last from Charleston, hath taken and subscribed the Oath of Allegiance and Fidelity to the Commonwealth of Pennsylvania, before Samuel Miles, Esquire, Mayor of the city of Philad'a, on this sixteenth day of August, 1790.

Robert Marshall, Mariner, son of John Marshall, of Belfast, of the Kindgom of Ireland, Husbandman, and Margaret, his wife, born in Belfast, aged twenty-three years, last from the Isle of Man, but now of the city of Philad'a, hath taken and subscribed the oath of Allegiance and Fidelity, to the Commonwealth of Pennsylvania before Samuel Miles, Esquire, Mayor of the said city, on the ninth day of September, 1790.

SAM'L MILES.

Inrolled, 27th April, 1791.

April 26, 1791. Gian Tilian, Market street, Philadelphia, Shopkeeper, took the oath of Allegiance and Fidelity prescribed by act of Assembly, passed the 4th March, 1786, this day, before me.

SAMUEL WHARTON.

Inrolled, 27th April, 1791.

The Oath of Allegiance to the Commonwealth of Pennsylvania hath been taken before Hilary Baker, one of the Aldermen of the city of Philadelphia, between the first day of October, 1790, and first day of October, 1791, by the following persons, viz:

July 11, 1791. John Coenrad Muysken, of the city of Philadelphia, Merchant, son of John Muysken, of Amsterdam Merchant and Catharine his wife born at Amsterdam and lately arrived here from Surinam.

August 23. Jean Jacques Favre (John James Favre), Watchmaker, son of Frederick Favre, of the town of Locle, in the county of Neufchatle, in Switzerland, Farmer, and Maria, his wife, born at the town of Locle, af'd, lately arrived here from the Province of Britany, in the Kingdom of France.

September 30.   Francis L. Campion, Merchant, son of Julian L. Campion, of Normandie, in France, Merchant, and Frances Clair, his wife, born at Mitchelle a Lapiere, in the province of Normandie, af'd, lately arrived here from the city of Rotterdam, in the United Provinces.   Witness my hand and seal, Philadelphia, first October, 1791.

HILARY BAKER. [SEAL.]

Inrolled, 1st October, 1791.

Duplicate.—I do certify that Lawrence Huron, of the city of Philadelphia, Merchant, hath voluntarily taken and subscribed the Oath of Allegiance and Fidelity, as directed by an act of General Assembly of Pennsylvania.   Witness my hand and seal the eleventh day of October, seventeen hundred and eighty-five.

JOHN GILL. [SEAL.]

Inrolled, the 20th March, 1795.

Oath of Allegiance, Andre Delago.

City of Philadelphia, ss: I, Matthew Clarkson, Mayor of the city of Philadelphia, do hereby certify that Andre Delago, Merchant, son of Etienne Delago, of St. John D'Agelie, in France did this day take and subscribe before me the Oath of Allegiance prescribed by an act of the General Assembly of the Commonwealth of Pennsylvania, passed the thirteenth day of March, 1789.

In testimony whereof I have hereunto subscribed my name and caused the seal of the said city to be affixed the second day of January, 1794.

MATTH. CLARKSON. [SEAL.]

Inrolled, the 27th of April, 1796.

Oath of Allegiance, Robert Gill.

I, Robert Gill, of the city of Philadelphia, and a citizen of the State of Pennsylvania, do swear that I will support the Constitution of the United States of America.

ROBERT GILL.

Sworn and subscribed the 4th day of Feb., 1797, before

THOS. McKEAN.

Inrolled the 4th day of Feb'y, 1797.

Oath of Allegiance, Manuel Revero.

August 4th, 1791.   There personally appeared before me, Gunning Bedford, one of the Aldermen of the city of Philadelphia, Manuel Revero, Mariner, his father was Casimero Revero, shipwright, of Havannah, from whence this deponent last arrived, and the said Manuel Revero, having arrived in this city last from Havannah, hath this day voluntarily taken and subscribed the Oath of Allegiance and Fidelity as directed by an act of General Assembly of Pennsylvania, passed the thirteenth day of March, 1789. Certifyed under my hand and seal the day and year first above written.

[SEAL.] GUNN'G BEDFORD.

Inrolled the 18th November, 1797.

We, the undernamed, do swear that we will be faithful and bear true allegiance to the Commonwealth of Pennsylvania as a free and independent State, and that we will not, at any time, willfully and knowingly do any act, matter or thing which will be prejudicial or injurious to the freedom or independence thereof.

R. Lachicotte Larague, from St. Domingo, aged thirty-four years and born in St. Domingo. Sworn the 13th February, A. D. 1794. Coram.

MATH'W IRWIN, *Commis.*

Francis Lefevre, from St. Domingo, born in Nantz, aged forty-nine years, son of Peter Lefevre. Sworn the 13th February, 1794. Coram.

MATH'W IRWIN, *Commis.*

Perce Maher, from the county of Kilkenny, aged about 24 years, son of John and Elizabeth Maher. Sworn 20th March, A. D. 1794. Coram.

MATH'W IRWIN, *Commis.*

John Anthony Paris, ✕ last from Havana, aged thirty-three years, born in Oporto, in Portugal, son of John and Mary Gonsalis, Paris. Sworn the 14th day of August, A. D. 1794 Coram.

His
mark.

MATH'W IRWIN, *Commis.*

Nicolas Louis Fontaine Defresnaye, from Paris, aged thirty years, son of Louis Fontaine Defresnaye and Marie Ann Rann. Sworn the 29th day of Novem'r A. D. 1794. Coram.

MATH'W IRWIN, *Com'r.*

James Cameron, from London, aged twenty-eight years, son of James and Bell Cameron, being a ship carpenter by trade and having resided here five years. Sworn the 5th February, A. D. 1795. Coram.

MATH'W IRWIN, *Com'r.*

John Lewis Fieron, from Valance, last from St. Domingo, arrived in this city the 4th May, 1792, since which time he has resided in this city, aged 29 years, son of John and Marguerite Gezin Fieron. Sworn the 16th February, A. D. 1795. Coram.

MATH'W IRWIN, *Com'r.*

James N. Taylor, from Londonderry, Ireland, arrived in this city in September, 1792, since which time he hath resided in this city, aged twenty-one years and upwards, son of Allen and Eleanor Taylor, who resided in Ireland. Sworn the 12th March 1795. Coram.

MATH'W IRWIN, *Com'r.*

We, the undernamed, do swear, that we will be faithful & bear true Allegiance to the Commonwealth of Pennsylvania as a free and independent State, and that we will not at any time wilfully and knowingly do any act, matter or thing which will be prejudicial or injurious to the freedom or independance thereof. [*This law passed 13 March, 1789.*]

John Bonnet. Sworn the 27th June, 1793. Coram.

MATH'W IRWIN, *Com'r.*

Lawren Hazard, gentleman from St. Domingo, Omer Lalon, from Paris, Louis de Noaillere, from St. Domingo. Sworn the 10th day of July, A. D. 1793. Coram.

MATH'W IRWIN, *Com'r.*

George Dougherty, born in Philadelphia, aged 28 years, ironmonger. Sworn the 20th September, A. D. 1793. Coram.

MATH'W IRWIN, *Com'r.*

Nicolas Antoine Gabriel Creuil, from Paris, aged thirty-six years. Sworn the 19th November, A. D. 1793. Coram.

MATH'W IRWIN, *Com'r.*

Charles Cosme Marie Meynard, from Clunes, in France, aged thirty-three years. Sworn the 19th November, A. D. 1793. Coram.

MATH'W IRWIN, *Com'r.*

Chs. McAllister, son of Chas. & Ezabellah McAllister, born in Scotland, aged twenty-nine years, mariner. Sworn the 27th November, A. D. 1793. Coram.

MATH'W IRWIN, *Com'r.*

List of persons who, between the first day of October, 1791, and the first day of October, 1792, before Hilary Baker, one of the Aldermen of the city of Philadelphia, took and subscribed the Oath of Allegiance and Fidelity to the Commonwealth of Pennsylvania, prescribed by a law of the said Commonwealth, enacted on the thirteenth day of March, Anno Domini, 1789, vizt:

January 18th, 1792. John Godfrey Wachsmouth, merchant, son of John Godfrey Wachsmouth, of Hamburg, in Lower Saxony, merchant, and of Anna Maria, his wife, born at Hamburg aforesaid, and arrived in the city of Philadelphia from Great Britain in the year one thousand seven hundred and eighty-four, took and subscribed the Oath of Allegiance afore-said.

April 12th. John Christian Kegel, cordwainer, son of John Christian Kegel, cordwainer, and Maria Magdalena, his wife, born in the City Halle, in Saxony, and arrived here about seven months since from London *via* Salem, in New England, took and subscribed the oath aforesaid.

June 16th. John Carrere, merchant, son of John Carrere of the Department of Vela Gironve, in the town of Lisburn, in the Kingdom of France, physician, and Mary Sibelat, his wife, lately arrived in the city of Philadelphia, from Bordeaux, in France, *via* Virginia, took and subscribed the oath aforesaid.

July 28th. Joseph Detchevary, mariner, born at Bourdeaux, in the Kingdom of France, son of Joseph Detchevary of Bourdeaux aforesaid, merchant, and Magdalen Fangars, his wife, and lately arrived at the city of Philadelphia from the Island of Hispaniola, took and subscribed the oath aforesaid.

August 31st. James Wetherald, mariner, born in the county of Yorkshire, in the Kingdom of Great Britain, son of James Wetherald of the county aforesaid, farmer, and of Margaret his wife, who arrived in the State of Pennsylvania about three years since from the Kingdom of Great Britain aforesaid, took and subscribed the oath aforesaid.   Witness my hand

HILARY BAKER.

List of persons who, between the first day of October, 1792, and the first day of October, 1793, before Hilary Baker, one of the Aldermen of the city of Philadelphia, voluntarily took and subscribed the Oath of Allegiance and Fidelity to the Commonwealth of Pennsylvania, prescribed by a law of the said Commonwealth, enacted on the thirteenth day of March, Anno Domini 1789, vizt:

October 12th, 1792. Alexander Dupuy, merchant, born at Rochelle, in the Kingdom of France, son of John Ellis Dupuy, late of Rochelle aforesaid, merchant, and Hariet, his wife, arrived about one year since at the city aforesaid from the Island of Hispaniola, took and subscribed the oath aforesaid.

October 30th. Joseph Darande, mariner, born at Marseilles, in the Kingdom of France, son of Gabriel Darande, of Marseilles farmer, and of Margarette, his wife, arrived at the city aforesaid from the Island of Hispaniola, took and subscribed the oath aforesaid.

November 15th, Alexander Loue, mariner, born at Nance, in the Kingdom of France, son of Francis Loue, of Nance aforesaid, merchant, and of Mary Cottenian, his wife last arrived at the city

of Philadelphia from the Island of Hispaniola, took and subscribed the oath aforesaid.

December 5th. Gabriel Xaviere Fyard, gentleman, son of
Louis Fyard, gentleman, premier precedent of Vasoul, and of
Ann, his wife, born at Vasoul, in the Kingdom of France, lately
arrived at the city aforesaid from St. Domingo, took and subscribed the oath aforesaid.

December 7th. John Perreau, son of Peter Perreau, of the
late province of Poitier, in the Kingdom of France, gentleman,
and Catharine, his wife, born at St. Ester, in the province of
Navarre, in the said kingdom, who hath for several years com-
manded vessels under American colours from the port of Philadelphia, and lately arrived at this city from the island of St.
Domingo, took and subscribed the oath aforesaid.

March 2. 1793. Abraham Lindo, Merchant, son of Elias Lindo,
late of the city of London, in the Kingdom of Great Britain,
Merchant, and of Grace, his wife, born at the city of London,
aforesaid, and arrived at the city of Philadelphia in March,
1792, from the island of Jamaica, took and subscribed the oath
aforesaid.

March 9th. John Shaw, Mariner, born in Queen's county,
in the kingdom of Ireland, son of John Shaw, of the county
aforesaid, Cotton Manufacturer, and Elizabeth his wife, lately
arrived at the city of Philadelphia *via* New York, from the city
of Dublin, in the Kingdom of Ireland, aforesaid, took and
subscribed the oath aforesaid.

March 10. Francis John Mary Vincent Gouro, Mariner, born
at Mahon, in the Kingdom of France, son of Mary Ann Francis,
Gouro, gentleman, and Pelagia Ann Marie, his wife, lately arrived at the city of Philadelphia, from St. Domingo, took and
subscribed the oath aforesaid.

March 10. John Wilson, Mariner, born in the city of Rotterdam, in Holland, son of William Wilson, of Rotterdam, aforesaid, Cooper, and Margaret, his wife, arrived at New York, from
Rotterdam about eight years since, and since that time sailed
from different ports in the United States, took and subscribed
the oath aforesaid.

March 26. Nicholas Gordon, Mariner, born at Marblehead,
in the State of Massachusetts, son of Samuel Gordon, late of
Marblehead, aforesaid, Sailmaker, and of Tabitha, his wife,
who has always hitherto sailed out of some of the ports within
the United States, and lately arrived here from Lisbon, took
and subscribed the oath aforesaid.

March 26. Leonard Baxter, Mariner, born at Weatherfield,
in the State of Connecticut, son of Elisha Baxter, of the same
place, Cordwainer, and of Rhoda, his wife, who has hitherto

always sailed out of some of the ports within the United States and lately arrived here from Lisbon, took and subscribed the oath aforesaid.

April 27, 1793. Barkle McClean, Mariner, born at Belfast, in the Kingdom of Ireland, son of George McClean, of the city of Dublin, gentleman, and of Margaret his wife, and who for eight years past has sailed in American vessels from and to the port of Philadelphia and other ports within the United States, took and subscribed the oath aforesaid.

May 1. Peter Newchatel, gentleman, residing in Moreland township, in Montgomery county, born at Rouen, in Normandie, in France, son of Peter Newschatel, of the same place, gentleman, and Marie Bimaut, his wife, and arrived at Philadelphia about one year since from Cape Francois, took and subscribed the oath aforesaid.

May 4th. Defondina Rubardo, Mariner and master of a vessel, born at Port Maurice, in Genoa, son of Francis Rubardo of Port Maurice, aforesaid, Merchant, and Joanna, his wife, who arrived here upwards of thirteen months last past from the Island of St. Thomas, and has since that time resided in the city aforesaid, took and subscribed the oath aforesaid.

May 6th. Timothy Russell, Mariner, a native of Belfast, in the Kingdom of Ireland, son of Michael Russell, late of Belfast, aforesaid, Mariner, and Ann, his wife, came in the Commonwealth of Pennsylvania to reside in the year 1785, and hath since that time resided in the said Commonwealth, took and subscribed the oath aforesaid.

May 6th. Robert Lewis, Jr., Merchant, born in Monmouth county, in the State of New Jersey, son of Nathaniel Lewis Esq., of the city of Philadelphia, and Lucy, his wife, and resided in the city of Philadelphia upwards of eight years last past, took and subscribed the oath aforesaid.

May 10th. James Porter, mariner, on his solemn oath deposeth, that he was born in Salem, in the State of Massachusetts, that he is the son of Thomas Porter, late of Salem aforesaid, mariner, and of Jemima, his wife, and that he hath not, since the Declaration of American Independence, been a citizen or subject of any State or kindgom other than of the said State of Massacuhsetts and of the United States of America, took and subscribed the oath aforesaid.

May 13th, 1793. Thomas Davies, mariner, on his solemn oath, doth declare that he was born in Middlesex county, in England, that he is the son of Howell Davies of the same county, gentleman, and of Jane, his wife, that for space of about seven years last past he sailed from and to divers ports within the United States, and that he married, and for three years last past resided in the said city of Philadelphia, took and subscribed the oath aforesaid.

May 22d.   Augustine Griffony, merchant, born at Grace, in Province in France, son of Gulliame Griffany, merchant, and Elizabeth, his wife, in Grace aforesaid, and lately arrived in at the city of Philadelphia from Cape Francois, took and subscribed the oath aforesaid.

May 23d.   William Muir, Merchant, born in Scotland, in the Kingdom of Great Britain, son of David Muir, of Scotland, aforesaid, merchant, and Christiana Parlone, his wife, and arrived in the United States from Amsterdam about six months since with intention of becoming a citizen of the State of Pennsylvania and of the United States, took and subscribed the oath aforesaid.

May 27th.   James Enefer, Mariner, born in the county of Suffolk, in the Kingdom of Great Britain, son of Samuel Enefer, of the county aforesaid, cordwainer, and of Mary, his wife, arrived at Philadelphia about three years since from the city of London, with intention of becoming a citizen of the State of Pennsylvania, took and subscribed the oath aforesaid.

May 27th.   John Bennett, Mariner, on his oath before me taken, Deposeth that he is the Son of Alexander Bennett of the State of Massachusetts, Farmer, and Mary, his wife, that he was born in the State of Massachusetts aforesaid, and that since the declaration of the Independence of the United States he has not been a Citizen or subject of any Prince or State other than the said State of Massachusetts and of the United States, took and subscribed the oath as aforesaid.

May 29th.   Andrew Clement Desenclosde Saint Laurent, Lieutenant of the Provost of the Parish of Gross Morne, in the Quarter of Port de Pai, in the Island of St. Domingo, Son of Nicholas Desenclosde Saint Laurent, Esqr., and Elizabeth Le Clere, his wife, of the City of Rouen, in Normondoien, France, and lately arrived at the City of Philadelphia, from Port de Paix, took and subscribed the oath aforesaid.

May 29th, 1793.   John Peter Prunet, late Attorney of the Jurisdiction of Cape Francois, in the Island of St. Domingo, in the French West Indias, Son of Peter Prunet, Merchant at Tarbes and Bigose, and Elizabeth Soubiran, his wife, and lately arrived at the City of Philadelphia, from Cape Francois, took and subscribed the oath aforesaid.

May 29th.   Robert Taylor, Mariner, Son of Richard Taylor, of Wickley County, in the Kingdom of Ireland, Cordwainer, and of Catharine, his wife, born in the County aforesaid, and arrived at Charlestown, in South Carolina, in the year 1782, since which time he considered himself as a Citizen of the

United States, and sailed from divers Ports in the United States, took and subscribed the oath aforesaid.

May 30th. Anthony Schwellenback, Palatin, Merchant, Son of Frederick Schwellenback, of Blankenberger, in the Dutchey of Bergen, in the Palatinate, Yeoman, and Elizabeth Maurer, his wife, both dec'd, lately arrived at the City of Philadelphia, from Cape Francois, in the Island of St. Domingo, took and subscribed the oath aforesaid.

May 30th. Emmanuel Limes, Merchant, son of Benot Limes, Merchant at Toulouse, in the province of Languedoc, deceased, and Martha Daupias, his wife, arrived at the City of Phila-delphia on the 5th day of May, Anno Domini, 1792, from Haver-de-Grace, took and subscribed the oath aforesaid.

June 1st. Charles Joseph Dieulourd, Merchant, son of Peter Dideulourd, of Doulins, in Picardy, in France, Merchant, deceased, and Mary Margaret Blondel, his wife, lately arrived at the City of Philadelphia from the Island of St. Domingo, took and subscribed the oath aforesaid.

June 1st. Lewis Hyppolite Delabarre, Attorney-at-Law, son of John Delabarre, of Neuilly St. Front in the Province of the Isle of France, Physican, and Mary Margaret Soyens, his wife, both deceased, lately arrived at the City of Philadelphia from the Island of St. Domingo, took and subscribed the oath afore-said.

June 1st, 1793. Saturnin Bernard Garrick, Merchant, son of Claudius Lawrence Garrick, of Marsailles, in France, Merchant, deceased, and Jane Souiller, his wife, arrived at the City of Philadelphia in the beginning of July, 1792, in the French Brig L'Federation, from Cape Francois, in the Island of St. Dom-ingo, took and subscribed the oath aforesaid.

June 3d. Peter Papon, Merchant, son of Francis Papon, of Ponilly Lesfaurs, in the province of Forest, in France, Gentle-man, and de St. Cyr, his wife, lately arrived at the city of Philadelphia, from Cape Francois, in the Island of St. Domingo, took and subscribed the oath aforesaid.

June 3d George Duxen, mariner, son of William Duxen, of Belfast, in the Kingdom of Ireland, Clerk, and of Mary, his wife, born at Kingsale, in Ireland aforesaid, arrived at Phila-delphia from the Island of Jamaica, about four years since, since which time he has sailed in American vessels from and to the Ports of Philadelphia and New York in the United States, took and subscribed the oath aforesaid.

June 5th. Lewis James Dumois, Merchant, Son of James Du-moise, of Montpellier, in France, Merchant, and of Jane Lucan, his wife, arrived at the City of Philadelphia, in the beginning of April last, from Port au Prince, in the Island of St. Domingo, took and subscribed the oath aforesaid.

June 5th. Anthony Vigne, Merchant, Son of Anthony David Vigne, of Nismes, in the Province of Languedoc, in France, Merchant, and of Elizabeth Saubeuan, his wife, arrived at the City of Philadelphia, on the ninth day of May, 1792, from Jeremie in the Island of St. Domingo, took and subscribed the oath aforesaid.

June 7th. Fusiens De Brey, Planter, born in the province of Picardy, in France, son of Charles De Bray, late of Picardy, aforesaid, yeoman, and of Mary Anne Dontard, his wife, lately arrived from Cape Francois, in the Island of St. Domingo, at the City of Philadelphia, took and subscribed the oath aforesaid.

June 8th, 1793. Jean Francis Boisbuille de Gazon, Gentleman, born in the Island of St. Vincent, Son of Perez Boisbuille De Gazon, of the Island of Martinique, Gentleman, and of Marie Greaux, his wife, arrived at Philadelphia on the twenty-fourth day of May, 1792, from the Island of St. Lucie, took and subscribed the oath aforesaid.

June 11th. Jean Baille, Merchant, born in the province and County Le Foix in France, son of Geraud Baille, of the same place, Farmer, and of Catharine, his wife, lately arrived in the City of Philadelphia from Cape Francois, took and subscribed the oath aforesaid.

June 11th. John McFail, Mariner, born in the District of Southwark, in the County of Philadelphia, Son of John McFail, late of Southwark aforesaid, Labourer, and Catharine, his wife, took and subscribed the oath aforesaid.

June 11th. Benjamin Kimpton, Mariner, born at Bedford, in the State of Massachusetts, Son of Benjamin Kempton, of Bedford aforesaid. Ship Carpenter, and Sarah, his wife, took and subscribed the oath aforesaid.

June 14th. Jean Baptiste de Mauret Lafaurie, Gentleman, born in the Island of Guadaloupe, son of Bernard Mauret, of the same place, Gentleman, and of Neau De Costier, his wife, lately arrived at Philadelphia from the said Island of Gaudaloupe, took and subscribed the oath aforesaid.

June 14th. Charles Louis De La Chauvetiere, Gentleman, born in the Island of St. Domingo, Son of Jean Etienne de la Chauvetiere de nive, and of Catharine, his wife, lately arrived at Philadelphia from the Island aforesaid, took and subscribed the oath aforesaid.

June 15th. Auguste Francois Des Champs, Gentleman, born at Cape Francois, in the Island of St. Domingo, Son of Francois Gabriel Des Champs, of the same place, Gentleman, and Marie, his wife, lately arrived at Philadelphia from Cape Francois aforesaid, took and subscribed the oath aforesaid.

June 18th. Armand Gabriel Francois Paparel La Boissier, at present of the City of Philadelphia, Gentleman, born at Cape Francois, in the Island of St. Domingo, Son of Claude Francois Paparel La Boissier, of the same place, Gentleman, and of Rabia, his wife, lately arrived at the said city from Cape Francois, took and subscribed the oath aforesaid.

June 18th, 1793. Jean Louis Du Crit, at present of the City of Philadelphia, Gentleman, born in the Province of Loraine, in France, Son of Peter du Crit, of the same place, Gentleman, and of Marie Vauderevey, his wife, lately arrived at the city aforesaid from Cape Francois, took and subscribed the oath aforesaid.

June 22d. Jean Louis Le Pilletere, Merchant, born at Cherberg, in Normandie, Son of Jean Francois Le Pelletere, of the same place, Gentleman, and of Mary Carpentier, his wife, lately arrived at the City of Philadelphia from New Orleans, took and subscribed the oath aforesaid.

June 22d. Charles Robin, Merchant, born at Tours, in France, Son of Maude Robin, of the same place, Gentleman, and of Louis Tayette, his wife, lately arrived at the City of Philadelphia from the Island of St. Domingo, took and subscribed the oath aforesaid.

June 22nd. Rene Baranger, merchant, born at Vilicers, in France, son of Pierre Baranger, of the same place, gentleman, and of Marie Salliot, his wife, lately arrived at the city of Philadelphia from the Island of St. Domingo, took and subscribed the oath aforesaid.

June 22nd. Francis Adrian Thibault, son of James Thibault, of Paris, in France, house builder, and of Angelique Harlo, his wife, both deceased, arrived at Philadelphia from Logane, in the French West Indies, in the month of June, 1792, in the schooner Le Patrie, Capt. Larrel, from Bordeaux, took and subscribed the oath aforesaid.

June 29th. Joseph Lacombe, officer during the late war between England, France and the United States, Son of John Lacombe, of Usset, in Limousin, in France, Gentleman, and Mary Ann de Perreaux, his wife, arrived at Philadelphia from Port au Prince, in the French West Indies, in the month of May last, took and subscribed the oath aforesaid.

July 3. Laurent Vidal, Mariner, born at Toulon, in France. Son of Etrienne Vidal, of the same place, Gentleman, and of Claire, his wife, lately arrived at the City of Philadelphia from New Orleans, took and subscribed the oath aforesaid.

July 5th, 1793. James Alexander de Fontaines, Gentleman, born at Cape Francois, Son of Alexander de Fontaines, of the same place, Gentleman, and of Marie Martha, his wife, lately arrived at Philadelphia from Cape Francois aforesaid, took and subscribed the oath aforesaid.

July 5th. Lewis Prudhomme, Junior, Merchant, born at Vizen, in Anjore, in, France, Son of Rene Prudhomme, of the same place, Gentleman, and of Magdalin, his wife, arrived at Philadelphia on the first day of May, 1792, from the Island of St. Domingo, took and subscribed the oath aforesaid.

July 12th. Joseph Hilary Carbonnel, Merchant, and son of John Francis Carbonnel, late of Marsailles, Gentleman, deceased, and of Magdalen Payne, his wife, lately arrived at the city of Philadelphia from Cape Francois, took and subscribed the oath aforesaid.

July 12th. James Chossen, Merchant, Son of Francis Chossen, of Marsailles, Merchant, and of Elizabeth Maurice, his wife, both deceased, lately arrived at Philadelphia from Cape Francois, took and subscribed the oath aforesaid.

July 12th. Peter Castets, Mariner, Son of Peter Castets, of Bourdeaux, Gentleman, and Mary Casemant, his wife, lately arrived at the City of Philadelphia from Cape Francois, took and subscribed the oath aforesaid.

July 12th. John Baptist Relion, Merchant, Son of Francois Relion, late of Bourdeaux, merchant, and of Ann Dupont, his wife, both deceased, lately arrived at the City of Philadelphia from Cape Francois, took and subscribed the oath aforesaid.

July 15th. Peter Bell, Mariner, born at Preston Panns, in Scotland, Son of James Bell, of the same place, mariner, and Susanna, his wife, who arrived at Philadelphia, about nine months since, from Amsterdam, took and subscribed the oath aforesaid.

July 15th. Henry Major, of the City of Philadelphia, Mariner, who, on his oath, declares that he is the son of Henry Major, Londonderry County, in Ireland, Farmer, and Ann, his wife, that he is now about twenty-one years old, that he became apprentice to his Brother Thomas Major, about eight years ago, who then was part owner of a vessel registered wholly as American property and traded Between New York and Londonderry, but Considered himself an Inhabitant of the State of New York, and that he, the said Henry, has ever since that time sailed in Vessels which were American Built or owned by Inhabitants of the United States, and that for two years last past, he sailed from and to the Port of Philadelphia, took and subscribed the oath aforesaid.

July 19th, 1793. James McElroy, of the City of Philadelphia, merchant, born in the County of Tyrone, in Kingdom of Ireland, Son of Bryan McElroy, of the same place, Farmer, and of Catherine, his wife, who, about one year since, arrived in the State of South Carolina, from Dublin, and about Three months since came to the city aforesaid, took and subscribed the oath aforesaid.

June 25th. Simon Brocas, Merchant, Son of John Brocas, of Nova Scotia, Merchant, deceased, and Mary Deselos, his wife, lately arrived from Charleston, South Carolina, where he has resided since the 12th June, 1792, at the City of Philadelphia, took and subscribed the oath aforesaid.

June 25th. Lewis Debescon, Merchant, Son of John Debescon, of Lagarde, in the province of Gascoyne, in France, Gentleman, and Martha Darmagnac, his wife, both deceased, lately arrived at the City of Philadelphia from Cape Francois, took and sub-scribed the oath aforesaid.

June 25th. Emmanuel Edmond Aimie Sassay, Merchant, Son of Peter Sassay, Merchant, of Magny, in the French vixin, and Elizabeth Ribault, his wife, both deceased, lately arrived from Cape Francois, at the City of Philadelphia, took and sub-scribed the oath aforesaid.

June 25th. Anthony Brus, Merchant, Son of Peter Brus, of Ax, in Providence of Gascony, Apothecary, and Margaret San-soube, his wife, lately arrived at the City of Philadelphia from Cape Francois, took and subscribed the oath aforesaid.

June 27th. William Record, Mariner, born at Boston, in the State of Massachusetts, Son of Peter Record, of Boston afore-said, Mariner, and of Catharine, his wife, who sailed for about three years last past from the Port of Philadelphia, and lately arrived at the said City from the Island of St. Bartholomew, took and subscribed the oath aforesaid.

June 27th. Thomas Cooper, Mariner, born in Stafordshire, in England, Son of William Cooper, of the same place, Tallow Chandler, and of Margaret, his wife, who for about three years last past sailed out of Ports within the United States, and on the eleventh inst. arrived at the City of Philadelphia from the Island of St. Martin's, took and subscribed the oath afore-said.

July 29th, 1793. William Ridge, Mariner, born at Charleston, in South Carolina, Son of William Ridge, of Charleston aforesaid, Tanner, and of Elizabeth, his wife, who sailed out of the Port of Philadelphia about eighteen months last past, and lately arrived from the Island of St. Martin's, took and subscribed the oath aforesaid.

August 8th. John Du Cornan, Merchant, born at Bayonne, in France, Son of James Du Cornan, of Bayonne, aforesaid, Mariner, and Anna Duhalty, his wife, lately arrived at Philadelphia from Cape Francois, in the Island of St. Domingo, took and subscribed the oath aforesaid.

August 9th. Patrick McDonald, Mariner, born at Laun, in the Kingdom of Ireland, Son of Patrick McDonald, late of Laun, aforesaid, Baker, dece'd, and of Mary, his wife, who has sailed to and from the United States upwards of ten years last past, and lately arrived at Philadelphia from Antigua, took and subscribed the oath aforesaid.

August 9th. Denis Terme, Merchant, born at Lyon, in France, son of Jacques Terme, of the same place, Gentleman, and of Antoinette, his wife, arrived about the latter end of April at New York from Port au Prince, in the Island of St. Domingo, and since arrived in the City of Philadelphia, took and subscribed the oath aforesaid.

August 12th. Arthur Higginbotham, Seaman, born at Innis Killen, in the Kingdom of Ireland, Son of Newbold Higginbotham, late of the same place, Clerk, deceased, and of Elizabeth, his wife, who since the year 1783 sailed from and to the port of Baltimore, in the State of Maryland, in vessels owned by inhabitants of the said State, and lately arrived at the City of Philadelphia from Baltimore, afs'd, took and subscribed the oath aforesaid.

August 14th. John Simon, Merchant, born at Tours, in France, Son of Matthew Simon, late of the same place, manufacturer, and Frances, his wife lately arrived at the City of Philadelphia from Cape Francois, took and subscribed the oath aforesaid.

August 14th. John Wilson, seaman, born at Leinster, in the Kingdom of Ireland, son of William Wilson, late of Leinster, aforesaid, Gardener, and of Margaret, his wife, and arrived at Philadelphia from Cape Francois on the eighth inst., took and subscribed the oath aforesaid.

August 14th, 1793. Laughlin McClain, Seaman, born at Greenock, in Scotland, from whence his Father, Hugh McClain, in the year 1782, emigrated with his Family when this Deponent was 14 years old, since which time he hath resided in the City of Philadelphia, and hath not since that time been a Citizen or subject of any State or County other than of the State of Pennsylvania and of the United States, took and subscribed the oath aforesaid.

August 17th. Mathew Rodes, Mariner, born at Bayonne, in France, Son of Joseph Rodes, of the same place, Mariner, and of Marie, his wife, lately arrived at the said City of Philadelphia from Cape Francois, took and subscribed the oath aforesaid.

August 19th. Joseph Michael Dieulafoy, Merchant, born at

Toulouse, in France, Son of Guillaume Michael Dieulafoy, of the same place, Gentleman, and of Marie, his wife, and arrived at Philadelphia on the twelfth day of June last from Cape Francois, in the Island of St. Domingo, took and subscribed the oath aforesaid.

August 24th. Anthony Paquin, Merchant, born in Alsace, Son of Joseph Paquin, of the same place, Merchant, and of Joanna, his wife, lately arrived at the City of Philadelphia from Cadiz, took and subscribed the oath aforesaid.

August 29th. Joseph Fitzpatrick, Starch and Gluemaker, born in the County of Clare, in the Kingdom of Ireland, Son of Daniel Fitzpatrick, of the County aforesaid, Farmer, and of Mary his wife, arrived in the City of Philadelphia on the nineteenth day of July, Anno Domini 1792, from Dublin, in Ireland, *via* in New York, took and subscribed the oath aforesaid.

August 31st. Peter Duvivier, Merchant, born at Tours, in France, Son of Peter Duvivier, of the same place, Merchant, and of France, his wife, arrived at Philadelphia in May, in 1792, from Cape Francois, took and subscribed the oath aforesaid.

August 31st. Stephen Dupuy, Mariner, born at Bourdeaux, in France, Son of Stephen Dupuy, of the same place, Mariner, and of Mary, his wife, arrived at Philadelphia aforesaid in May, 1792, from Cape Francois, took and subscribed the oath aforesaid.

September 3rd, 1793. Louis Nicholas Mansard, Merchant, born at Beauvais, in Picardy, in France, Son of Jean Mansard, of the same place, Gentleman, and of Marie, his wife, arrived at the city of Philadelphia in the Beginning of August, in the year 1792, from Cape Francois, and hath ever since sojourned within the State of Pennsylvania and the neighbouring States, took and subscribed the oath aforesaid.

September 4th. Jean Andre Barbaroues, Sen'r, Gentleman, born at Valin province in France, Son of Jean Baptist Barbarouse, of the same place, Gentleman, and Elizabeth, his wife, who arrived about eighteen months since at Boston from Nantz, in France, hath since that time resided in the United States, and hath purchased real estate in the city of Philadelphia, took and subscribed the oath aforesaid.

September 4th. Guilliaume Francois Dumenit, Merchant, born at Havre de Grace, in France, Son of Jean Dumenit, of the same place, merchant, and of Mary, his wife, arrived at Philadelphia on the sixteenth day of July last, from Cape Francois, took and subscribed the oath aforesaid.

September 4th. Jean Dubarry, merchant, born at Dantist, in Bigore, son of Gabriel Dubarry, of the same place, Gentleman, and of Elizabeth, his wife, arrived at the City of Philadelphia on the eighth day of August last from the Island of St. Domingo, took and subscribed the oath aforesaid.

September 5th. Armand Caignet, Gentleman, son of Armand Caignet, of Loogane, in the West Indies, Gentleman, and of Mary, his wife, born at Cape Francois, and arrived at Philadelphia from Cape Francois on the sixth day of May, 179-, took and subscribed the oath aforesaid.

September 6th. William Penrose, Mariner, born at Hull, in England, Son of John Penrose, of the same place, Bricklayer, and of Sarah, his wife, arrived about three years ago at the City of Philadelphia from the City of London, took and subscribed the oath aforesaid.

Witness My Hand,

HILARY BAKER.

List of Persons who, between the thirteenth day of September‡ 1793, and first day of October, 1794, before Hilary Baker, one of the Aldermen of the City of Philadelphia, took and subscribed the oath of Allegiance and Fidelity to the Commonwealth of Pennsylvania, enacted on the thirteenth day of March, Anno Domini one thousand seven hundred and eighty-nine, vizt:

November 6, 1793. Samuel Lewis, accountant, born in the City of New York, Son of John Lewis, late of the said City, surveyor, deceased, and Mary, his wife, lately arrived at the City of Philadelphia, from the City of London.

November 18th. Jean Baptist Icard, Merchant, born at Liberne, in France, Son of Jean Icard, of the same place, merchant, and of Marguerite, his wife, arrived at Philadelphia, about six months since, from Port au Prince.

November 25th. Stephen Greffen, merchant, born at Venice, in Italy, Son of Peter Greffen, of Venice aforesaid, mariner, and of Antonia, his wife, arrived at the City of Philadelphia from New Orleans, in the month of September, Anno Domini one thousand seven hundred and ninety-one.

November 26th. Charles Parmentier, Merchant, born at Bruges, in the Austrian Netherlands, son of Anthony Parmentier, of the same place, Merchant, and of Isabella Debades, his wife, arrived at Philadelphia in the month of September last from the Island of Martinique.

December 6th. Nicholas Scheppers, Merchant, born at Lisle, in French Flanders, Son of Nicholas Scheppers, late of the same place, Merchant, deceased, and of Maria Teresia, his wife, arrived at the City of Philadelphia from New Orleans in the month of August, in the year of our Lord one thousand seven hundred and ninety-two.

December 9th. Pierre Andre Ravon, Merchant, born at Angouleme, in France, Son of Nicholas Ravon, of the same place,

Cloth Manufacturer, and of Marie, his wife, arrived at Philadelphia in the month of October last from the Island of St. Domingo.

December 9th. Andrew Barclay, Mariner, born at Edenburgh, in Scotland, Son of William Barclay, of the City of London, Clerk, and of Margaret, his wife, arrived about five years since at Virginia from London, and about two years last in and near the City of Philadelphia in the Commonwealth of Pennsylvania.

December 11th. Edward Harris, Seaman, born at Hampshire, in Great Britain, Son of Michael Harris, of the same place, Cooper, and of Catharine, his wife, who arrived at New York, in the year 1780, from the City of London, and hath since that time resided in and sailed from and to different Ports in the United States, and for about six years last past resided in and sailed from and to the City of and Ports of Philadelphia, and is married and settled there as the Head of a Family upwards of two years last past.

December 11th. John Downs, Seaman, born at Hampshire, in Great Britain, Son of Wm. Downs, of the same place, Farmer, and of Amelia, his wife, who about three years since arrived at New York from Poole, in Great Britain, and hath since that time sailed in American vessels from and to American Ports, and during two years last past from and to the Port of Philadelphia.

December 16th. Francis McGonnigle, seaman, born in the County of Donegal, in the Kingdom of Ireland, Son of Peter McGonnigle, of the same place, Farmer, and of Sarah, his wife, who arrived at Philadelphia about ten years since, and hath since that time Constantly sailed in American vessels from and to the port of Philadelphia, and now hath a family at Philadelphia.

December 16th. Nicholas de la Newville, Music Master, born at Metz, in France, son of Nicholas de la Newville, of the same place, Gentleman, and of Charlotta, his wife, who arrived at Philadelphia from Paris in the month of February, in the year 1790, and that since that time resided in the City of Philadelphia, and now hath a family in the said City.

December 18th. James McCutcheon, Mariner, born in the district of Southwark, in the County of Philadelphia, Son of James McCutcheon, late of the same place, victualler, dece'd, and Elizabeth, his wife, who hath always resided in and near the City of Philadelphia.

December 18th. David Williamson, Mariner, born in the City of New York, Son of Joseph Williamson, at present at the City of Philadelphia, Glazier, and Mary his wife, who hath from his infancy resided in or near the City of Philadelphia.

July 24th, 1794. Louis Gobert, merchant, born at Bellefant, in the province of Limaze, in France, son of Baptist Gobert, of the same place, Gentleman, and Mary, his wife, who on the twenty-eighth day of December, 1792, arrived at Baltimore from Jeremia or St. Domingo, and arrived at Philadelphia from Baltimore in September last.

July 26th. John Baptist Riviere, merchant, born at the City of Bordeaux, in France, Son of Pierse Riviere, of the same place, merchant, and Margaret, his wife, who in the month of June, 1793, arrived at the City of Philadelphia from Louisiana.

July 28th. Thomas Croft, Mariner, born in the City of London, in Great Britain, Son of Thomas Croft, of the same City, Broker, and Elizabeth, his wife, arrived at Philadelphia from London, aforesaid, in the year 1781.

August 4th. Vincent Ghirardini, Fruitseller, born at Mantua, in Italy, Son of Julius Ghirardini, Counsellor-at-law, and Eleonora, his wife, arrived at New York the second day of July, 1784, from the City of Orleans, in France, and about seven years since came from thence to the City of Philadelphia.

August 1st. Francis Vence, merchant, born at Marseilles, in France, Son of Michael Vence, of Marseilles aforesaid, merchant, and of Delphine, his wife, arrived the fifth day of July last at Philadelphia, from the Island of St. Eustatia.

August 9th. Daniel Ace, Mariner, born at Swansey, in South Wales, in England, Son of Thomas Ace, of the same place, Labourer, and Helen, his wife, who, for the thirteen years last past, hath sailed from and to the ports of the United States in vessels owned by American Citizens, and the last five years of the said Term from and to the ports of Philadelphia.

August 12th. Louis Francis Brun, Merchant, born at Cape Francois, in the Island of St. Domingo, Son of Andrew Brun, of the same place, Mason, and of Marie Anne, his wife, in the month of March last past, arrived at the City of Philadelphia, *via* New York, from Carthagenia.

September 4th. William Beynroth, merchant, born at the City of Brunswick, in Germany, Son of Ernst Peter Beynroth, late of the same place, Gentleman, deceased, and of Juliana, his wife, who arrived here from Philadelphia *via* Baltimore, from Bremen, in the month of July, 1793.

September 13th. John Aires, Seamen, about 27 years old, born in Guinea, that in his infancy he was kidnapped by White Ruffians and Carried away from his native Country to St. Croix, that he was there sold, and became the slave of John Braun, of Copenhagan, Merchant. That about nine years since the said John Braun gave him his freedom, and that upwards of five years since he suffered Shipwreck and was taken from the wreck by Capt. Weekes, and brought to the City of Philadelphia.

September 22d. James Long, the younger, mariner, born at Cork, in the Kingdom of Ireland, Son of James Long, of Cork, aforesaid, mariner, and of Mary, his wife, in the month of March, 1793, arrived at Philadelphia, from Cork Aforesaid.

December 23d. James Pede, Mariner, born at Norfolk, in Virginia, Son of James Pede, of the same place, Tallow Chandler, and of Margaret, his wife, who has sailed from and to the port of Philadelphia in American vessels for about ten years last past, and lately arrived at Philadelphia aforesaid from Bristol, in Great Britain.

December 25th. John Welsh, Ropemaker, residing with his Family in the district of Southwark, in the County of Philadelphia, appeared this day in his proper Person, and of his solemn oath declares he was born at Boston, in the State of Massachusetts, that he is the son of John Welsh, late of Boston aforesaid, Cordwainer, deceased, and of Margaret, his wife, that about seventeen months ago he removed with his family from Norfolk, in Virginia, to Southwark aforesaid, and hath since that time resided there, and that since the Declaration of Independence of the United States he has not been either a Citizen or subject of any State or nation other than the United States.

December 25th. Robert Denniston, Ropemaker, living in Southwark, in the County of Philadelphia, born at Port Glassgow, in Scotland, Son of Robert Denniston, of Port Glassgow aforesaid, Ropemaker, and of Ann, his wife, arrived at Philadelphia about twenty months since from Greenock, in Scotland, since which time he has resided in Southwark aforesaid.

Jan'y 16th, 1794. Charles McAllister, Mariner, born in the shire of Argyle, in the Kingdom of Great Britain, Son of Charles McAllister, of the same place, Farmer, and Isabella, his wife, who about five years since arrived at the City of Philadelphia from the Island of Jamaica, since which time he has constantly resided in the said City of Philadelphia.

February 8th. John William Faussat, Merchant, born at Bourdeaux, in France, Son of John Faussat, of Bourdeaux aforesaid, Merchant, and of Mary, his wife, who in the month of November, in the year of our Lord, 1792, arrived in the City of Philadelphia from the Island of St. Domingo, and hath since that time resided in the said City of Philadelphia.

February 13th. John Maria Soullier, Merchant, born at the City of Auch, in France, Son of Peter Soullier, of the same place, Merchant, and of Maria Anne, his wife, who in August last arrived at the City of Philadelphia from Cape Francois, and hath since that time resided in the said City.

February 13th, 1794. James Mathieu, Merchant, born at Lourmarine, in France, son of Stephen Mathieu, of Lourmarine, aforesaid, Merchant, and of Magadalin, his wife, arrived at the City of Philadelphia from Cape Francios on the twenty-fifth day of October. 1792.

February 19th. Thomas Shorthouse, Merchant, born at Birmingham, in Great Britain, Son of Thomas Shorthouse, of the same place, Chemist and Druggist, and of his wife, arrived from Great Britain at New York on the eighth day of June, 1791.

February 22nd. Charles Francis Deslandes, Gentleman, born at Cherberg, in Normandie, Son of Francis Deslandes, of the same place, Gentleman, and of Mary, his wife, arrived at Philadelphia about three months since from the Island of St. Domingo.

March 11th. Arnaud Desaa, Gentleman, born at Bayonne, in France, son of Benoit Desaa, Gent., and of Marie Guirana, his wife, of Bayonne, aforesaid, arrived at Philadelphia from Cape Francois on the twenty-fourth day of May, 1792.

March 22d. Jacob Harrison, Clerk, born at Leeds, in England, Son of Robert Harrison, of Leeds, aforesaid, merchant, and of Ann, his wife, arrived at Philadelphia about two years since from Liverpool, in Great Britain.

March 28th. John Pinder Sanderson. Merchant, born in the City of York, in Great Britain, Son of John Sanderson, late of the said City, Merchant, dece'd, and of Abegail, his wife, arrived at the City of Philadelphia in the month of September, 1791.

April 4th. James Henderson, of the City of Philadelphia, merchant, born in the shire of Perth, in Great Britain, Son of Thomas Henderson, late of the same place, Merchant, dece'd, and of Helen, his wife, arrived from Great Britain in the year 1772, since which time he has resided within the United States, and about ten years last past in the said City of Philadelphia.

April 4th. William Holderness, of the City of Philadelphia, merchant, born at Fangfoss, in the County of York, in Great Britain, Son of Francis Holderness. late of the same place, House Carpenter, deceased, and Jane, his wife, arrived at Boston from Great Britain, in the year 1775, since which time he has resided within the United States, and since November, 1791, in the City of Philadelphia.

May 13, 1794. Michael Nicholas, merchant, born in Boiney, in Normandie, in France, Son of Michael Nicolas, of the same place, Laborer, and of Marie Louise, his wife, arrived at Philadelphia, from Havre de Grace, in the month of July, 1791.

May 14. Magloire Dehogues, Gentleman, born at Loches, in France, Son of Urban Dehogues, of the same place, Gentleman, and of Catherine, his wife, arrived at Philadelphia, from Fort Dolphin, in the Island of Hispaniola, on the second day of November, 1793.

May 16th. Thomas Taylor, Mariner, born at Greenock, in Scotland, Son of James Taylor, of Greenock aforesaid, mariner, and of Margaret, his wife, arrived at Philadelphia, near seven months since, from Bristol, in England.

May 16th. Joseph Larelle, mariner, born at Bourdeaux, in France, Son of John Larelle, of the same place, merchant, and of Margaret, his wife, arrived at Philadelphia, about two years since, from Cape Francois.

May 17th. Josuah Naar, merchant, born at Curassoe, Son of David Naar, of Curassoe, merchant, and of Sarah, his wife, arrived at Philadelphia about ten months since, from Cape Francois.

May 19th. John Pierre Morgan, merchant, born at Membrow, in Dauphiney, in France, Son of Francis Morgan, of Membrow aforesaid, Gentleman, and Marie, his wife, arrived at Philadelphia about six months since, from Cape Francois.

May 21st. George Vannest, Blockmaker, born in the City of Philadelphia, where he hath always resided, Son of Peter Vannest, of the same City, Laborer, and of Elizabeth, his wife.

May 21st. Isaac Sennef, Blockmaker, born in the City of New York, Son of George Sennef, late of the City of Philadelphia, Taylor, deceased, and of Mary, his wife.

May 21st. John Sample, Mariner, born near Newry, in Ireland, Son of Samuel Sample, formerly of Newry aforesaid, but late of Philadelphia, Mariner, deceased, and of Margaret, his wife, arrived at Philadelphia with his parents in his infancy.

May 23d. John Stewart, Mariner, born in the Isle of Bute, in Scotland, Son of Alexander Stewart, of the same place, Mariner, and of Mary, his wife, arrived at Philadelphia about two years since from the Island of Jamaica.

June 3d. John Smyth, Merchant, born at Madaira, Son of William Smyth, of the same place, Merchant, and of Ann, his wife, who about twenty-five months since arrived at Wescasset, in the State of Massachusetts, from Dublin, and on the tenth day of June last at Philadelphia.

June 21st. John Brown, Mariner, born in the City of London, in England, Son of John Brown, late of the same place. Cabinetmaker, deceased, and of Isabella, his wife, arrived at Philadelphia about eleven years since from London aforesaid, with

6—VOL. III.

John Simson, of Philadelphia, Mariner, to whom he was bound apprentice at London.

June 25th. Ralph Mather, Merchant, born near Manchester, in England, Son of Thomas Mather, late of the same place, Farmer, deceased, and of Mary, his wife, arrived at Philadelphia in November, 1792, from Liverpool, in England *via* New York.

June 26th. Joseph Powers, Mariner, born in Stafordshire, in England, Son of John Powers, late of the same place, Coachman, deceased, and of Ann, his wife, arrived at Philadelphia about three months since from the Island of Providence *via* Savannah, in Georgia.

June 26th. Bartholomew de Ronchamp, Gentleman, born at St. Jean Angelis, in the Province of St. Onges, in France, Son of Peter Bartholomew de Ronchamp, of the same place, Provost General in the armies of France, and of Marie Ann, his wife, who in the month of August last arrived at the City of Philadelphia from the Island of St. Domingo.

July 2d. John Malder, Seaman, born in the City of Hamburg, in lower Saxony, son of John Malder, late of the same place, Labourer, dece'd, and of Dorothy, his wife, arrived at Philadelphia about three years since, from Bristol in England.

July 15th. Pedro Ramon De la Porta Bringes, Gentleman, born at Barcelonia, in the Knigdom of Spain, Son of Peter Delier Porte, Lieutenant Colonel in the armies of Spain, and of Cecelia, his wife, of Barcelonia, aforesaid, arrived at Philadelphia on the eighteenth day of May last, from the Island of Bermudas.

July 17th. Lawrence Derick, Seaman, born at Dunkirk, in France, Son of Jacob Derick, late of the same place, Miller, dece'd, and of Isabella, his wife, arrived at Nantuckett, about three years since, from Dunkirk, and lately at Philadelphia, from the Island of Martinique.

July 17th. Anthony Sanches, mariner, born on the Island of Minorca, Son of Anthony Sanches, of Minorca aforesaid, Carpenter, and of Francisca, his wife, arrived in February, 1793, at Philadelphia, from New Orleans.

July 17th. Samuel Liburn, Mariner, born in the Island of Bermudes, Son of Rich'd Liburn, late of the same Island, mariner, dec'd, and of Sarah, his wife, arrived at Philadelphia about four months since, from Norfolk, in Virginia.

July 21st. George Roche, merchant, born at Limerick, in Ireland, Son of Stephen Roche John, of the same place, merchant and of Margaret, his wife, arrived at Philadelphia in June last, from the Island of St. Eustatia.

July 23d. Alexander Hays, mariner, born at Edenton, in North Carolina, Son of Thomas Hays, of the same place, Stonecutter, and of Margaret, his wife, lately arrived at Philadelphia, from the State of South Carolina.

July 24th. Severe Raveille, merchant, born at Agde, in Languedoc, in France, Son of Charles Raveille, of the same place, Notary, and of Christine, his wife, arrived at Philadelphia, in August, 1792, from the Island of St. Domingo.

Before me,

HILARY BAKER.

List of Persons who have taken the oath of Fidelity and Allegiance to the Commonwealth of Pennsylvania, time of taking the oath, Persons' Names, Occupation, Place of Nativity, Parents' Names, Place from whence they last came:

June 2d, 1789. George Elliot, Sailor, Richmond, in Virginia, Father, John, Mother, Elizabeth, London.

July 2d. William Cox, Sailor, Parish of Devonshire, Island of Bermudas, Father, John, Mother, Martha, Antigua.

July 16. Antoin Germain Chardon, Nantz in Old France, Father, Germain, Mother, Care, Nantz.

May 1st, 1790. James Tullock, Sailor, Inverness, in Scotland, Father, James, Mother, Elizabeth, Port au Prince.

May 1st. Daniel Church, Sailor, Salem, New England, Father, Joseph, Mother, Deborah, Port au Prince.

May 13th. Joseph Morris, Sailor, Waterford, Ireland, Father, Edward, Mother, Mary, Waterford.

November 10. William Atten, Sailor, Liverpool, England, Father, George, Mother, Eleanor, Liverpool.

November 10. Alex'der Lawler, Sailor, county of Wexworth, Ireland, Father, Thomas, Mother, Margaret.

April 10th, 1793. Robert Lee, Sea Captain, Berwick upon Tweed, in Scotland, Father, John, Mother, Elizabeth, Berwick.

May 1st. Peter Dominick Robert, Merchant, Marseilles, in France, Father, Peter Kessu, Mother, Susanna, Cape Francois.

May 2nd. Peter Kifrelelain, Merchant, Isle of Rhe.

May 6th. James John Mazura, Merchant, Low Britain, in France, Father, Joseph, Mother, Mary Pitot, Brest.

May 23d. James Mathwein Bensist, Merchant, Anjau, France, Province, Port au Prince.

May 23d. Bartholomew Corvisier, Merchant, Renes, Province of Britainy, Father, Francois, Mother, Gilbert Desprees, Port au Prince.

June 18th. Thomas Wilkey, Sea-faring man, Newport, Rhode Island, Father, Thomas, Mother, Mary, Newport.

December 20th. James Rowin, Trader, County of Rowan, Ireland, Father, William, Mother, Sarah, Londonderry.

March 20th, 1794. Archibald McVair, Sailor, Cambleton, Scotland, Father, Duncan, Mother, Margaret.

March 20th. John Shaw, Sailor, Scotland, Father, Angus, Mother, Jane, Glasgow.

City of Philadelphia, ss :

I do Certify that the foregoing is a true list of all the Persons who have taken the oath of Fidelity and Allegiance to the Commonwealth of Pennsylvania before me. Witness my hand and seal this ninth day of April, 1794.

JOSEPH SWIFT, *Alderman.* [SEAL.]

REMONSTRANCE OF INHABITANTS OF CHESTER COUNTY AGAINST THE TEST LAW.

FEBRUARY 17th, 1787.

To the Honorable the representatives of the freemen of the Commonwealth of Pennsylvania, in General Assembly met:

The Petition and remonstrance of a number of the inhabitants of the County of Chester humbly sheweth:

That your petitioners observe that by a Law passed the 4th day of March, 1786, entitled an Act for securing to this Commonwealth the Fidelity and Allegiance of the inhabitants thereof, and for admitting certain persons to the rights of citizenship, the oath prescribed is not only an oath of Allegiance, but also of abjuration and retrospection, against the two parts of which oath last mentioned your Petitioners would remonstrate, subjoining their Reasons.

1st. As to the Retrospective part. Admiting that a part of the inhabitants of this State have joined, aided, assisted & abeted the Fleets & Armies of the King of Great Brittain, knowing them to be such, is that a sufficient reason for excluding them from the benefits of citizenship? Now, if the appeal is made to policy, we answer no, the disclaiming the Idea of retaining a number of Alien enemies to Government dispersed through the Territories of that Government, and that the prevention of the participation of the common rights of freemen has a tendency to alienate the affections is a fact that will not we apprehend be contended. If to Justice the answer will be that the burthens of Govermnent ought to be imposed equally upon all the community, and that the non-jurors are exempted from a proportionable part by not serving as Jurors, Assessors, &c., will be readily admited. If to the Constitution, the Bill of Rights declares that no part of a man's property can be justly taken from him or applied to public uses, without his own consent or that of his legal representatives. And the frame of Government that every freeman of the full age of twenty-one years, having resided in this State for the space of one whole year next before the day of Election for representatives, and paid public Taxes during that time, shall enjoy the right of an Elector.

2d. As to the abjuration part, we would simply observe that

an oath of Allegiance is in fact abjuring all other Governments, and that the abjuration becomes a mere nullity, but as it has a tendency to detract from our national character by giving rise to the idea that our independency is yet insecure, we remonstrate against it.

Your Petitioners therefore pray that a Law may be passed repealing such parts of the Oath as directed by the Law passed the 4th of March, 1786, as requires an Abjuration of the King of Great Britain, and also that part which takes a retrospective view, and your Petitioners, as in duty bound, will ever pray.

ARCHIBALD AGNEW,
THOS. ALLEN,
WILLIAM HACKET,
JAMES ALLEN,
CHARLES GRIMES,
JAMES HALL,
ANDREW McANTIER,
ALEXANDER McINTIRE,
JAMES BELL,
SAMUEL MILLER,
WILLIAM MOORE,
JOHN WHITTING,
JOSHUA FOULKE,
JOHN MORRISON,
GEORGE STOREY,
JOHN MILLER,
JOSEPH MILLER,
ROBERT BOOTHE,
GEORGE STARR,
GEO. EVANS,
AND'W HENDERSON,
HUGH WILLSON,
JOSHUA PINEY,
WM. PUSAY,
OLIVER RUSSELL,
JOHN RUSSELL,
JOHN WILLIAMS,
DAVID RODGERS,
SAMUEL McINTIRE,
WM. WILSON,
THOMAS SHARP,
HUGH RUSSELL.

INDEX